T0316518

Cambridge Elements ≡

Elements in the Global Middle Ages
edited by
Geraldine Heng
University of Texas at Austin
Susan Noakes
University of Minnesota, Twin Cities

LATE TANG CHINA AND THE WORLD, 750–907 CE

Shao-yun Yang
Denison University

CAMBRIDGE
UNIVERSITY PRESS

Shaftesbury Road, Cambridge CB2 8EA, United Kingdom

One Liberty Plaza, 20th Floor, New York, NY 10006, USA

477 Williamstown Road, Port Melbourne, VIC 3207, Australia

314–321, 3rd Floor, Plot 3, Splendor Forum, Jasola District Centre, New Delhi – 110025, India

103 Penang Road, #05–06/07, Visioncrest Commercial, Singapore 238467

Cambridge University Press is part of Cambridge University Press & Assessment, a department of the University of Cambridge.

We share the University's mission to contribute to society through the pursuit of education, learning and research at the highest international levels of excellence.

www.cambridge.org
Information on this title: www.cambridge.org/9781009397254

DOI: 10.1017/9781009397278

First published 2023

A catalogue record for this publication is available from the British Library.

ISBN 978-1-009-39725-4 Paperback
ISSN 2632-3427 (online)
ISSN 2632-3419 (print)

Cambridge University Press & Assessment has no responsibility for the persistence or accuracy of URLs for external or third-party internet websites referred to in this publication and does not guarantee that any content on such websites is, or will remain, accurate or appropriate.

Late Tang China and the World, 750–907 CE

Elements in the Global Middle Ages

DOI: 10.1017/9781009397278
First published online: May 2023

Shao-yun Yang
Denison University

Author for correspondence: Shao-yun Yang, yangs@denison.edu

Abstract: In recent decades, the Tang dynasty (618–907) has acquired a reputation as the most "cosmopolitan" period in Chinese history. The standard narrative also claims that this cosmopolitan openness faded after the An Lushan Rebellion of 755–63, to be replaced by xenophobic hostility toward all things foreign. This Element reassesses the cosmopolitanism-to-xenophobia narrative and presents a more empirically grounded and nuanced interpretation of the Tang empire's foreign relations after 755.

Keywords: Battle of Talas, An Lushan Rebellion, xenophobia, Sinographic sphere, Late Tang dynasty

ISBNs: 9781009397254 (PB), 9781009397278 (OC)
ISSNs: 2632-3427 (online), 2632-3419 (print)

Contents

Introduction

In recent decades, the Tang dynasty (618–907) has acquired a reputation as the most "cosmopolitan" period in Chinese history – a period, we are told, when the Chinese people built an immense empire that connected East and West via the Silk Road, welcomed visitors and immigrants from around the world, and enthusiastically integrated other cultures into their own. Numerous accounts of Tang history also claim that this cosmopolitan openness faded after the An Lushan Rebellion of 755–63, to be replaced by ethnocentric or xenophobic hostility toward all things foreign. This interpretation of the late Tang can be traced back as far as Arthur F. Wright's (1913–76) studies in the 1950s on the history of Chinese Buddhism. Here, for example, is a passage from a paper that Wright delivered to a conference of Sinologists in Paris in 1956 and subsequently published in the *Journal of Asian Studies* in 1957: "After the An Lushan rebellion, T'ang self-confidence and governmental effectiveness were not fully restored. The cosmopolitanism of the great days of T'ang slowly gave way, under the influence of barbarian attack and internal decay, to a cultural defensiveness which occasionally broke out into xenophobia."[1]

Wright used the cosmopolitanism-to-xenophobia narrative to explain what he saw as a growing rejection of Buddhism (a religion introduced from India) by the late Tang elite. This interpretation was subsequently popularized in the 1960s and 1970s by other influential Western Sinologists, including Edward H. Schafer, Jacques Gernet, and John K. Fairbank, and became entrenched in English-language treatments of Tang history.[2] In the Sinophone world, a similar grand narrative has become common and can be traced to articles published by the Taiwan-based historian Fu Lo-ch'eng (Fu Lecheng, 1922–84) in 1962 and 1972.[3]

In this Element, I would like to present a more nuanced and empirically grounded revisionist interpretation of the late Tang empire's foreign relations. What follows is technically a sequel to the Element *Early Tang China and the World, 618–750 CE*, in which I traced the Tang empire's rise and expansion into Inner Asia and the Korean peninsula in the seventh century, followed by its struggles to hold its new frontiers against the Tibetan empire, the Korean kingdom of Silla, and revolts by the Turkic and Khitan peoples. But the approach that I take here also exists in a state of both tension and complementarity with a larger message that I sought to convey in *Early Tang China and the World*: namely, that we need to think more critically about the fabled

---

[1] Wright, "Buddhism and Chinese Culture," 37.

[2] For details, see Yang, "Tang 'Cosmopolitanism.'"

[3] These are reprinted in Fu, *Han Tang shilun ji*, 209–26, 339–82.

cosmopolitanism of the early Tang and recognize that it was never as free of imperialist violence and ethnocentric attitudes as the popular image would have us believe. Despite modern historians' tendency to interpret the Tang as an early model or epitome for the mode of economic and cultural globalization that has so shaped their lives, it was not in fact a champion of open, unrestricted interaction and commerce with foreign countries. But if the early Tang was not as unequivocally open to the world as has often been claimed, neither was the late Tang significantly more antagonistic toward foreign peoples and cultures than the early Tang had been. In other words, modern historiography has exaggerated both early Tang cosmopolitanism and late Tang xenophobia to an extent unsupported by the historical evidence; there was neither a golden age of openness, nor a precipitous descent into anti-foreign isolationism. An informed exploration of Tang cultural history has to start with challenging both of these myths, not just one of the two.

This Element is organized into thematic sections, but along roughly chronological lines. The first two sections concern the professionalization of the Tang frontier armies and the geopolitical background to the well-known but much misunderstood Battle of Talas, in which the armies of the Tang empire and the Islamic caliphate clashed for the only time in history. The subsequent two sections consider the causes and consequences of the An Lushan Rebellion, with an emphasis on debunking the notion of a xenophobic turn in late Tang society. Section 5 argues, too, that a brief period of persecution of Buddhism and three other "foreign" religions by the imperial state in the 840s should be understood primarily in terms of Buddhist–Daoist rivalry, rather than xenophobia. Section 6 takes up the subject of the Tang empire's role in the formation of a distinct "Sinographic" cultural sphere in East Asia, as well as the question of why that sphere did not extend further north, south, or west. The Conclusion explains how the Tang empire finally collapsed and what effect this event had on the peoples on its frontier periphery.

1 The Transformation of the Tang Frontier Military

By the beginning of the eighth century, the Chinese empire had recovered its Anxi (Pacifying the West) Protectorate in the Tarim Basin from the Tibetans, while abandoning its conquests in Korea and Liaodong and ceding hegemony over the Mongolian steppe to the resurgent Eastern Türks. The chronically fractious tribes of the Western Türks, too, had broken free of Chinese suzerainty (which had been exercised through unpopular client khagans) and transferred their loyalty to the new Türgesh khaganate.[4] These geopolitical developments took place during the rule of the only female emperor in Chinese history, Wu

---

[4] For details on these events, see Yang, *Early Tang China and the World*, Section 5.

Zhao (r. 690–705[5]), who had begun her political career as consort of the third Tang emperor Gaozong (Li Zhi, r. 649–83[6]) and gone on to found her own dynasty, the Zhou. In 705, Wu – formerly invincible in court politics but now ailing at the age of eighty-one – was forced into retirement by a palace coup that restored the Tang to power for another two centuries. She died, of natural causes, later that year.

The restored Tang dynasty soon sought to regain Its former dominance in the western Turkic lands of Central Asia. In 708, an attempt at allying with the Tibetans to destroy the Türgesh backfired spectacularly, as the Türgesh khagan *Saqal (Suoge) learned of the plan and preemptively invaded the Tarim Basin, capturing the Anxi Protectorate's headquarters at Kucha.[7] Saqal pulled out after the Tang court appeased him by recognizing him as khagan of the Western Türks, but he was later attacked, captured, and killed by the Eastern Türks in 710–2. In the ensuing chaos, the Tang client khagan Ashina Xian captured the Türgesh capital Suyab and gained the submission of some of the Western Türk tribes. But Türgesh fortunes revived under the charismatic *Suluk (Sulu, r. 716–38), who retook Suyab from Ashina Xian and secured Tang recognition as a khagan in 719. Tang relations with Suluk remained volatile thereafter, as he cultivated an alliance with the Tibetans and periodically attacked the Four Garrisons of the Anxi Protectorate.[8]

During the first half of the eighth century, the Tang responded to this challenging geopolitical environment by gradually developing a new and more effective (if expensive) approach to frontier defense. Previously, ad hoc expeditionary armies had been assembled out of a mixture of prefectural garrisons, regimental headquarters (*zhechong fu* or *fubing*, essentially a hereditary military reserve force), new conscripts, and contingents levied from *jimi* ("bridled") polities. The new defense system divided the frontiers into permanent centralized commands, each responsible for defending an entire

---

[5] Wu's original given name is unknown; after becoming emperor, she adopted the name Zhao, written with a newly created character. She was given various posthumous titles, including Great Sagely Empress Zetian; Chinese historians generally call her Wu Zetian.

[6] Tang emperors are typically known by their posthumous ancestral temple names (e.g., Gaozong); the main exception was Wu Zhao, who was not posthumously recognized as a legitimate emperor and thus did not receive a temple name. I will follow this convention but also supply each emperor's given name on first mention. Numerous emperors changed their names at least once; I will opt for the name that an emperor used at the time of his death.

[7] Conjectural reconstructions of non-Sinitic ethnonyms, names, and titles in this Element are marked with an asterisk on first appearance. Modern Mandarin readings of the transliterations are provided in parentheses.

[8] Suyab was officially one of the Four Garrisons from 692 to 719, replacing Agni (Yanqi), even though the Türgesh captured Suyab in 703. In 719, the Tang finally acknowledged Suyab's loss by reverting to the original list of Four Garrisons: *Shulik (Shule, Kashgar), Khotan, Kucha, and Agni. See Shang, "Tang Suiye yu Anxi sizhen."

region (e.g., the Gansu Corridor, the Tarim Basin, or the Sichuan Basin) and headed by a military commissioner (*jiedushi*).[9] Each command had a large standing army of professional soldiers who were typically paid in grain and silk collected as tax from both their frontier region and the interior provinces. With an advantage over the old expeditionary armies in cohesion and familiarity with local terrain, the frontier armies were oriented toward deterring and repelling enemy raids. But they might also engage in punitive expeditions at the military commissioner's discretion, for which they could be supplemented by short-term peasant conscripts if necessary. These expeditions could be aimed at major adversaries like the Tibetans or Türgesh, but they were more often aimed at rebellious *jimi* client polities (e.g., those of the Khitans). While the frontiers had stabilized since 699, the Tang did continue to create *jimi* polities where possible and had accumulated some 800 by 742, more than twice the total of 331 regular prefectures.[10]

By 742, there were a total of ten regional commands, with close to half a million troops in all. The majority of the officers and soldiers were Chinese men from a peasant or convict background, but in the northern and northwestern commands, they also included significant numbers of immigrants from the Inner Asian frontier and the *jimi* polities, including Khitans, *Margat (Mohe/ Malgal),[11] *Tegreg (Tiele),[12] and Eastern Türks. Many were drawn by the promise of good pay in resources that they would otherwise have to raid for; others came to the Tang as refugees from war and unrest in Inner Asia, and found (somewhat ironically) that there was a good market for warriors on the Chinese side of the frontier; yet others were originally captives who had been taken into the empire against their will. In a relatively meritocratic military culture, immigrant professionals who had mastered the key skills of mounted archery and tactical maneuver could rise to the top through ability and ambition, regardless of their ethnicity or country of origin. As of 750, the military

---

[9] For a visual overview of the frontier regions, see Yang, *Frontiers of the Tang and Song Empires*, Maps 6a–6i, at https://storymaps.arcgis.com/stories/0cf798877457406fa5719b97ccfc5454#ref-n-Ar2rKw. For more on the transformation of the Tang military system, see Graff, *Medieval Chinese Warfare*, 189–92, 205–13. On *jimi* polities, see Yang, *Early Tang China and the World*, Section 3.

[10] *ZZTJ* 215.6847; *XTS* 43b.1120.

[11] My use of *margat* as the original form of the ethnonym follows Christopher Atwood. The Sinographic transcription of the ethnonym is read as *mohe* in modern Mandarin and *malgal* in modern Korean. It would have been *matgat* in the Middle Chinese of Tang times.

[12] I have followed the most commonly accepted reconstruction of the original Turkic form of the ethnonym rendered in medieval Chinese sources as 鐵勒 or 敕勒 (read in modern Mandarin as *tiele* and *chile*). However, Chen Ken has recently made a strong case, using epigraphic evidence, that the original written form in Chinese was 鐵勤 or 敕勤 (*tieqin* and *chiqin* in Mandarin), and that the Turkic form should thus be *Terigin*. This position may, in time, become widely accepted in the field. Chen, "Chile yu Tiele."

commissioner for the Anxi Protectorate was Gao Xianzhi (Kor. Go Seonji, d. 756), a descendant of Goguryeo aristocrats resettled on the northwestern frontier after the Tang conquest of their kingdom in 668.[13] Gao commanded the Anxi army in a famous battle with Abbasid Muslim forces in 751, the subject of Section 2. His counterpart on the Qinghai frontier, *Qoshu (Geshu) Han (d. 757), was the son of a Türgesh noble who had served as deputy protector-general of Anxi and married a Khotanese princess. Two Turco-Sogdian cousins, An Sishun (ca. 690–756) and An Lushan (703–57), served as military commissioners for the Ordos and Hebei frontiers respectively and carried on a feud of sorts with Qoshu Han.[14] It was An Lushan whose rebellion against the imperial court in 755 (the subject of Section 3) put an end to a fifty-year period of stability on the frontiers and is often seen as a turning point in Tang history.

2 The Battle of Talas (751 CE)

In 741, a letter from the Sogdian king of Chach (Tashkent) arrived at the court of Emperor Xuanzong (Li Longji, r. 713–56). In stilted Chinese, obviously translated from the Sogdian language, it read:

> Your slave has been loyal to the [Tang] state for a thousand generations, just like the Türgesh khagans in the days when they were loyal and their tribes peaceful and stable. Later, when they betrayed the Celestial Khagan, fire broke out beneath their feet. Now the Türks [again] belong to the Celestial Khagan.[15] The only threat in the west is the Arabs, and they are no stronger than the Türks. I prostrate myself and beg for your heavenly grace: do not abandon the Türk tribes; attack and break the Arabs. Then all countries will naturally return to peace and stability.[16]

The king made his appeal to Xuanzong at a time when the Sogdian states' long struggle against Arab Muslim domination had been plunged into uncertainty by the collapse of their military ally, the Türgesh khaganate.[17] After khagan Suluk's assassination by one of his lieutenants in 738, civil war had broken out among the Türgesh. This allowed the Tang military commissioner for the Tarim and Dzungarian basins to invade the Türgesh lands in 739, eliminating two of the three warring factions in the process.[18] As the Türgesh khaganate fell into disarray and Tang forces moved in to install a Western Türk aristocrat as

---

[13] On the Tang conquest of Goguryeo in 668, see Yang, *Early Tang China and the World*, Section 4.

[14] I use the term "Turco-Sogdians" to refer to Sogdian families that settled in the Türk khaganates and became culturally Turkicized as a result: see ibid., Section 3.

[15] On the origin of the title Celestial Khagan, see ibid., Introduction.

[16] *THY* 99.1772, with emendations based on *QTW* Chapter 999.

[17] For historical background and analysis of the Arab invasions of Sogdiana, see Haug, *The Eastern Frontier*, 89–92, 115–19, 122–37.

[18] Beckwith, *The Tibetan Empire in Central Asia*, 118–20; *ZZTJ* 214.6833–34, 6838.

"khagan of the ten tribes," the people of Chach apparently hoped that the Tang emperor could be persuaded to replace Suluk as their champion against the Arabs.[19]

The Sogdian king of Ushrusana also sent a letter to Xuanzong in 745. After similarly avowing his family's longstanding loyalty to the Tang, he asked the "Celestial Khagan" to treat Ushrusana as "a small prefecture of the Tang" and to command him, "your slave," to attack the empire's enemies.[20] The enemies of whom the king spoke were almost certainly the Arabs. Indeed, if Xuanzong ever wanted a war with the Umayyad caliphate (Figure 1), 745 would have been a perfect time to pursue it. Not only had Tang influence returned to the western Turkic heartland in the Ili River basin, but the Eastern Türk khaganate had also fallen in 741–5 due to infighting within its ruling elite and a revolt by the Uighur, Karluk (Geluolu), and Basmyl (Baximi) peoples, which received support from the Tang. The Uighurs, after winning a short war with the Basmyls, had founded a new steppe khaganate that pursued friendly relations with the Tang.[21] For the first time in over sixty years, the Tang faced no major threats from the Turkic world on both its northern and western frontiers. It was seemingly well placed to divert military resources toward liberating its vassals in Sogdiana. And though Xuanzong could not have known this, Muslims in Central Asia would soon be in a state of turmoil. The second revolt of Al-Harith ibn Surayj (d. 746), a former ally of Suluk and the king of Chach, broke out in early 746. It was shortly followed by the Abbasid Revolution, which began in Khurasan in 747 and overthrew the Umayyad caliphate in 750.[22] Under such circumstances, the Arabs would have been hard-pressed to hold Sogdiana against a determined assault by Tang troops based in the Tarim Basin. A Tang invasion that threatened Khurasan might even have changed history by preventing or at least delaying the Abbasids from launching their revolt in the first place.

But Xuanzong was unmoved by the Sogdian rulers' appeals to his authority as Celestial Khagan. This was not the first time in his long reign that he had chosen not to intervene in Sogdiana. In 719, the kings of Samarkand and Bukhara had already appealed to him for military aid in a revolt against the

---

[19] The Tang-installed khagan, Ashina Xin, was murdered in 742 by the Bagha Tarkhan (Mohe Dagan), the same man who assassinated Suluk. Tang forces killed the Bagha Tarkhan in 744 and appointed another Türgesh leader as "khagan of the ten tribes." *ZZTJ* 214.6841, 6843, 215.6854, 6860.

[20] *THY* 98.1754, with emendation based on *CFYG* 977.11312–13. The Tang knew Ushrusana as the kingdom of Cao. Its capital was located near modern Bunjikat, Tajikistan, and is today a major archaeological site.

[21] The Basmyls and Uighurs beheaded the last two Eastern Türk khagans and sent their heads to Xuanzong as a gesture of goodwill. *ZZTJ* 215.6844, 6854–55, 6860, 6863.

[22] See Haug, *The Eastern Frontier*, Chapter 6.

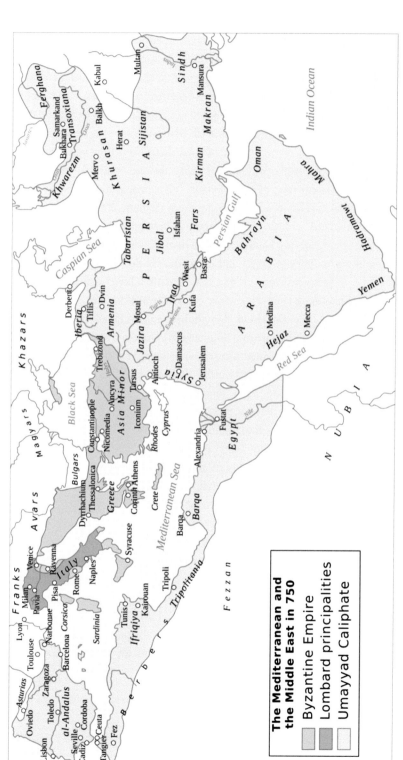

Figure 1 The Umayyad caliphate in 750. (Source: Wikimedia Commons)

Arabs, who had invaded them in 708–12 and forced them to start paying the *jizya* tax required of all non-Muslim subjects.[23] In 715, the Anxi Protectorate had indeed intervened militarily in a civil war in the kingdom of Fergana, defeating a ruler who had reportedly been installed with Tibetan and Arab military support. This precedent probably led the Sogdian states to believe the Tang would intervene on their behalf as well. Instead, Xuanzong ignored their pleas. In fact, the Anxi protector-general had dispatched troops to Fergana without the emperor's authorization, believing this necessary to prevent it from becoming a client state of the Tibetans.[24] Xuanzong himself never saw the Arabo-Islamic empire as a threat to the Tang frontier. Whereas Suluk did come to the Sogdians' aid, doggedly waging campaigns from 720 to 737 to drive the Muslims out of Sogdiana and Tokharistan, Xuanzong came to view the Türgesh leader's military strength and close ties to the Tibetans (including marriage to a Tibetan princess) as the real threat to Tang control over the Tarim and Dzungarian basins. Xuanzong even tried making an alliance with the Arabs to destroy Suluk in 734–6, though these efforts failed in the end.[25]

Rather than expand his empire into Sogdiana to compete with the Arabs after Suluk's death, Xuanzong remained focused on competing with the Tibetans. In fact, he became obsessed with recovering Shibaocheng (the "Stone-Walled Fort"), a strategically located and famously defensible Qinghai fortress. Shibaocheng had vertical cliffs on three sides and was accessible only via a narrow, winding road through the mountains; the Tang had taken it in 729 but lost it to the Tibetans in early 742.[26] Attack after attack failed to recapture the stronghold until some 63,000 troops from four Tang regional commands finally succeeded in 749, after military commissioner Qoshu Han threatened to execute their commanders unless they produced results in three days. Tens of thousands of Tang soldiers are said to have died in the process, many of them crushed by rocks and logs thrown from the ramparts.[27]

Qinghai was not the only front for Tang operations against the Tibetans in the 740s, as the mountains of what is now northern Pakistan had become a new arena of competition between the rival empires. The Tibetans had successfully asserted suzerainty over the statelets of Lesser Bolor (Ch. Xiao Bolü, modern Gilgit) and Greater Bolor (Ch. Da Bolü, modern Baltistan) in 734–5, raising Tang concerns that they would serve as staging points for Tibetan incursions

---

[23] *ZZTJ* 212.6735; *CFYG* 999.11558.

[24] *ZZTJ* 211.6712–13. See also the detailed analyses of the Fergana intervention in Beckwith, *The Tibetan Empire*, 75–83, 89–91; Wang, *Tang, Tufan, Dashi*, 147–50.

[25] Yang, "What Do Barbarians Know of Gratitude?", 60–68.   [26] *ZZTJ* 213.6784.

[27] *ZZTJ* 214.6846, 215.6868, 6878–79. 6896; Yang, *Frontiers of the Tang and Song Empires*, Map 6, 6b, at https://storymaps.arcgis.com/stories/0cf798878745406fa5719b97ccfc5454#ref-n-Ar2rKw.

into the western Tarim Basin.[28] At least three invasions of Lesser Bolor by the Anxi Protectorate failed to get past a heavily defended Tibetan outpost in the Pamirs. But in 747, an Anxi expeditionary force finally overran the outpost, entered Lesser Bolor, captured the king and his Tibetan queen, and executed the kingdom's pro-Tibetan faction. A garrison of up to 3,000 Anxi troops stayed behind to ensure that the next king would be acquiescent to Tang interests.[29] A similar expedition in 750 invaded Kashkar (Qieshi, modern Chitral in Pakistan), captured its king, and replaced him with his brother. This operation was instigated by a ruler in Tokharistan, who reported to Xuanzong that his enemy, the king of Kashkar, was hosting a Tibetan garrison and preventing the kingdom of Kashmir from providing supplies to the Tang garrison in Lesser Bolor.[30]

Later in 750, Tang troops from the Anxi Protectorate finally did arrive at Chach – not to defend it from the Arabs, but to sack it in another punitive expedition. The troops were led by Gao Xianzhi, the Anxi military commissioner himself; Xianzhi had also led the Lesser Bolor and Kashkar expeditions and had become known to the Arabs as "the lord of the mountains of China."[31] According to an Arabic source, the Anxi army was intervening in a conflict between Chach and neighboring Fergana (Figure 2). The reasons for this conflict are not recorded, but some Tang sources suggest that Chach had aligned itself with a "renegade" Türgesh khagan who was hostile to the Tang. In contrast, Fergana had aided the Tang intervention in the Türgesh civil war and remained a dependable proxy for Tang interests afterwards, earning its king a Tang princess in marriage in 744.[32] As for why Chach, whose king had fervently declared his loyalty to the Tang in 741, would be allied with an anti-Tang Türgesh faction by 750, one can surmise that Xuanzong's indifference to the Arab threat to Chach had forced the king to turn elsewhere for support.

The sack of Chach is the only known case of a Tang military attack on a state in Sogdiana, but it was not even a conventional siege or assault. Gao Xianzhi first deceived the king of Chach with a treaty of friendship and then seized his capital when the gates were opened. He plundered the city of its fabled wealth in gold and emeralds, massacred all "old and weak" inhabitants, and took the rest

---

[28] Wang, *Tang, Tufan, Dashi*, 181–82. For a map of the region, see Yang, *Frontiers of the Tang and Song Empires*, Map 6, 6g, at https://storymaps.arcgis.com/stories/0cf798878745406fa5719b97ccf c5454#ref-n-Ar2rKw.

[29] *ZZTJ* 215.6884–6886; *JTS* 104.3203–05, 109.3298; *XTS* 221b.6251–52; Beckwith, *The Tibetan Empire*, 130–33; Wang, *Tang, Tufan, Dashi*, 182–84.

[30] *CFYG* 999.11559–11560; *THY* 99.11773; *ZZTJ* 216.6897–98; Beckwith, *The Tibetan Empire*, 135–36.

[31] Beckwith, *The Tibetan Empire*, 136. Xianzhi was deputy military commissioner during the Lesser Bolor expedition and was promoted to military commissioner as a reward for its success.

[32] Bi, "Daluosi zhi zhan," 15–24; Beckwith, *The Tibetan Empire*, 137–38.

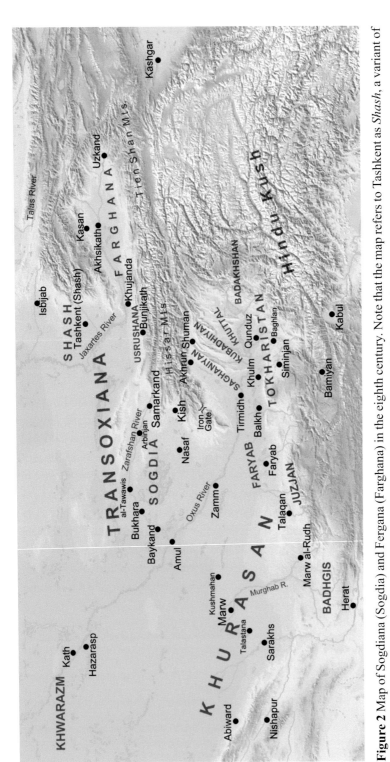

Figure 2 Map of Sogdiana (Sogdia) and Fergana (Farghana) in the eighth century. Note that the map refers to Tashkent as *Shash*, a variant of *Chach*. (Source: Wikimedia Commons)

prisoner, most likely to be sold into slavery.[33] In early 751, Xianzhi arrived in Chang'an to present Xuanzong with a group of high-level captives: the king and queen of Chach; the "renegade" Türgesh khagan; and the king of Kashkar. Xuanzong had the king of Chach beheaded in his presence, an unusually harsh punishment for a defeated ruler. Gao Xianzhi was rewarded with two honorific titles and permitted to keep his loot, becoming a rich man overnight.[34]

One of the princes of Chach had escaped its fall and fled to another Sogdian state, most likely Samarkand, where he told the tale of Gao Xianzhi's treachery. The outraged Sogdian audience, apparently now resigned to seeing the Arabs as the lesser of two evils, called upon Ziyad ibn Salih, the Abbasid governor of Sogdiana, to avenge the people of Chach. Ziyad assembled a large army, including reinforcements from Khurasan and Tokharistan, and advanced past Chach to occupy Talas (Taraz, Kazakhstan); Tang sources claim that his next target was the Four Garrisons, though he would probably have marched on Fergana or Suyab first.[35] Gao Xianzhi, now back in Kucha, marched to meet the Arab army with some 20,000 to 30,000 men. These included most of his Anxi troops as well as allied contingents recruited from Fergana and from the Karluks, who had migrated into the Ili River basin after 745 and replaced the Türgesh as the dominant Turkic group there. Chinese sources state that after a five-day standoff near Talas, the Karluks – perhaps perceiving that a Tang victory wouldn't be in their interest – changed sides and joined the Arabs in routing the Anxi troops. Xianzhi escaped with only a few thousand of his men, who reportedly had to fight their way through panicked Ferganan troops blocking their retreat.[36] Xianzhi was soon removed from his command and reassigned to the imperial guards in Chang'an.

The Battle of Talas, being the only major clash between the Chinese and Arabo-Islamic empires, has assumed legendary stature in modern historical narratives as an event that determined that Islam, not Sinitic civilization, would dominate Central Asia. A recent book on the Abbasid caliphate goes so far as suggesting that "were it not for Talas, Tehran and much of the Iranian world could well be speaking Chinese today."[37] But some historians have rightly argued that Talas was not the decisive turning point it is often thought to be.[38] The Anxi army was quickly rebuilt with new recruits, as seen from the

---

[33] *JTS* 104.3206, 109.3298.   [34] *ZZTJ* 216.6901, 6904; *THY* 79.1772.

[35] No extant source states the size of the Abbasid force. Recent claims, mostly made on the Internet, that a Tibetan army fought on the Arab side are false and unsupported by any primary source.

[36] Beckwith, *The Tibetan Empire*, 138–39; *ZZTJ* 216.6907–08; *JTS* 109.3298–99; Yang, *Frontiers of the Tang and Song Empires*, Map 6, 6h, at https://storymaps.arcgis.com/stories/0cf798878745406fa5719b97ccfc5454#ref-n-Ar2rKw.

[37] El-Hibri, *The Abbasid Caliphate*, 42.

[38] For example, Wang, *Tang, Tufan, Dashi*, 177–79. The Battle of Tours/Poitiers (732) has received similar demythologizing treatment since the beginning of the twenty-first century, after long being credited with saving Europe from Islamization.

successful punitive attack that it made on Greater Bolor in 753, so the losses at Talas did not permanently cripple the Anxi Protectorate.[39] In fact, even after sending their best troops to fight the An Lushan Rebellion in 756 and being cut off from outside support and reinforcement after 765, the Four Garrisons were still able to fend off Tibetan attacks until the 780s or 790s. The main reason why Tang forces in Anxi did not seek a rematch with the Abbasids was that, as we have seen, Xuanzong simply had no desire to confront the Arabs. There was no lack of opportunity to do so: In 752, the kings of Ushrusana, Bukhara, and nine other Central Asian states petitioned Xuanzong to join them in military action against the Abbasids, no doubt believing that he would now be eager to avenge his army's defeat. Again, they were wrong: Xuanzong merely humored them and took no action.[40] Many modern narratives identify Talas as the event that ended the Tang empire's westward expansion. This misses the fact that the Tang had already stopped expanding westwards for ninety years since the *jimi* system's purely symbolic extension across Sogdiana and Tokharistan.[41]

Any advantages that the Arabs gained through Talas were limited as well. Although the Tang defeat did enable Abbasid expansion into Chach and possibly Talas, even Fergana remained beyond firm Arab control until the early ninth century. Nor did the Abbasids gain dominance in the former Türgesh lands (including Talas and Suyab), which were instead taken over by the Karluks. The conversion of the western Turkic peoples and the western Tarim Basin to Islam only began in the tenth century, under the Karakhanid dynasty (believed to be partly descended from Karluks), and had little to do with the direct consequences of Talas.[42] It was also once believed that Chinese papermakers were captured in the battle and taken to Samarkand, where they then introduced paper to the Islamic world. But this story, first attested in an Arabic source from the tenth or early eleventh century, is most likely a myth. Papermaking techniques adapted from the Chinese method already existed in Central Asia, including Samarkand, before 751 and likely deserve the real credit for paper's spread into western Eurasia.[43]

We know that soldiers in the Anxi army were indeed captured by the Arabs at Talas, though certainly not the 20,000–25,000 prisoners claimed by Arabic accounts (which inflate the size of the Tang army to 100,000). One of them, named Du Huan, returned to China in 762 and wrote a geographical account with descriptions of Central Asia, the Islamic world, the Byzantine empire, and

---

[39] *ZZTJ* 216.6920–21.   [40] *THY* 98.1754; *XTS* 221b.6245.
[41] See Yang, *Early Tang China and the World*, Section 5.
[42] Hua, "Central and Western Tianshan"; Tor, "The Islamization of Central Asia."
[43] Bloom, *Paper Before Print*, 8–9, 42–45; *pace* Hyunhee Park, who takes the story at face value: Park, *Mapping the Chinese and Islamic worlds*, 25–26, 209 n. 18.

Sri Lanka. This text, which probably draws on both firsthand observation and information collected secondhand, has not survived, but numerous quotes are preserved in an early ninth-century encyclopedia by its author's relative Du You (735–812), who explains: "My junior clansman Huan went on a western expedition with Gao Xianzhi, the military commissioner of Zhenxi [i.e., Anxi], and reached the western sea in the tenth year of the Tianbao era [751]. At the beginning of the Baoying era [762–3], he returned home on a merchant ship via Guangzhou and composed the *Travel Record [Jingxing ji]*."[44]

Besides containing the first relatively accurate description of Islamic practices in Chinese, Du Huan's account reveals that in Kūfa, the Abbasid capital in 749–62, there lived immigrant Chinese silk weavers, goldsmiths, silversmiths, and painters whom Du credited (probably erroneously) with introducing their crafts to the Arabs. He even names two of the painters ("Fan Shu and Liu Ci, men of Jingzhao [Chang'an]") and two weavers of *luo* silk gauze ("Yue Huan and Lü Li, men of Hedong [Shanxi]").[45] How these men came to Iraq remains a puzzle. Some scholars have assumed them to be prisoners of war like Du Huan.[46] But Tang armies typically did not take professional artists and weavers on campaign, and professional soldiers would not have possessed the specialized leno weaving skills needed for making silk gauze. There is a strong possibility that the Chinese artists and artisans in Kufa had left Guangzhou on Arab or Iranian merchant vessels, in violation of Tang laws against private travel abroad, because they knew their skills in Chinese-style craftsmanship were in high demand overseas and would be generously remunerated.

3 The An Lushan Rebellion and Its Consequences

In the winter of 755, the military commissioner An Lushan rebelled against the Tang court at Youzhou (modern Beijing) and marched on Chang'an with troops from the Fanyang (northern Hebei) and Pinglu (Yingzhou area) regional commands, as well as allied contingents from the nomadic peoples of the northeastern frontier – reportedly 100,000 men in total.[47] Xuanzong considered this a stunning betrayal by a man whom he had repeatedly favored with promotions since 741, culminating in authority over an unprecedented three regional

---

[44] *TD* 191.5199. Du You does not explicitly state that Du Huan was a prisoner of war, perhaps because Huan found this embarrassing. A study and translation of the extant fragments of the *Travel Record* can be found in Akin, "The *Jing Xing Ji* of Du Huan."

[45] *TD* 193.5280. Alain George argues that the text is ambiguous as to whether these artisans were in Kūfa or just in the general region of Iraq: George, "Direct Sea Trade," 611.

[46] For example, Park, *Mapping the Chinese and Islamic Worlds*, 26; Pelliot, "Des Artisans Chinois."

[47] *ALS* 94. Later sources estimate Lushan's army at 150,000 strong and say that he claimed its strength to be 200,000: for example, *ZZTJ* 217.6934.

commands (Fanyang, Pinglu, and Hedong) on the northern frontier. The man responsible for Lushan's revolt seems to have been the chief minister Yang Guozhong (d. 756), a parvenu who owed his position to family ties and resented Lushan's open disdain for his political inexperience. Guozhong had been relentlessly investigating Lushan's associates and kin in the capital while attempting to convince Xuanzong that he had treasonous intentions. Some Tang sources claim that although Xuanzong remained skeptical, Lushan was indeed planning to rebel after Xuanzong's death, and that even his cousin Sishun knew of these plans and reported them to Xuanzong. Given the sources' evident bias and ex post facto rationalization, however, it is likely that Lushan remained loyal to the Tang until deliberately provoked into rebellion by Guozhong, who overconfidently anticipated his enemy's swift downfall at the hands of loyal Tang armies.[48]

Lushan was unable to mobilize troops from the Hedong command for his revolt, but such was the dearth of credible military forces in the imperial heartland that the Fanyang and Pinglu armies still overran Hebei and Henan without meeting significant opposition, then captured Luoyang after handily defeating an army of 60,000 raw conscripts (Figure 3). Lushan had initially declared an intent to remove Yang Guozhong from power, ostensibly on secret orders from Xuanzong. But taking the eastern capital so easily apparently stirred bigger ambitions in him, while news that Xuanzong had executed his eldest son Qingzong – who was a minister at the Chang'an court and had only recently married an imperial clanswoman – enraged him into acting on those ambitions. On the first day of the lunar year in 756, Lushan proclaimed himself emperor of a new Yan dynasty at Luoyang. His army advanced on Chang'an but was stalled at the highly defensible Tong Pass, guarded by more than 100,000 hastily assembled loyalist troops under Longyou military commissioner Qoshu Han.[49] In July, Xuanzong and Yang Guozhong unwisely forced Qoshu Han to lead his army out of the fortifications and fight a pitched battle; the rebels then lured the loyalists into a cleverly laid ambush in a gully and cut them to pieces.[50] Xuanzong and his court abandoned their now defenseless capital and fled south to the Sichuan Basin, but, en route, the soldiers escorting them turned on

---

[48] *ALS* 90–93; *ZZTJ* 216.6918, 217.6922–25, 6929–34, 6957.

[49] Qoshu was in Chang'an recuperating from a stroke when the rebellion broke out. Gao Xianzhi, too, was in Chang'an as an imperial guard general when the rebellion began. Xianzhi was first given overall command of the capital's troops and sent to engage the rebels, but he retreated to hold Tong Pass after the fall of Luoyang. He was soon executed on false charges of corruption and defeatism. Qoshu Han was then appointed to take his place, despite objecting that his physical condition would prevent him from exercising effective command. See *ZZTJ* 217.6932, 6937–40, 6942–44.

[50] *ALS* 102–103; *ZZTJ* 218.6966–69.

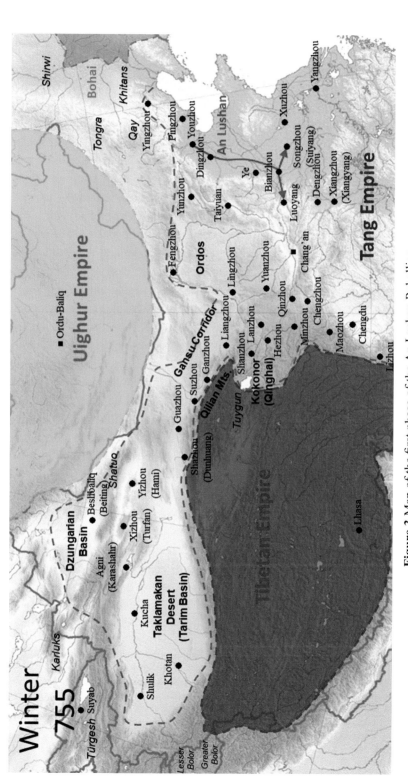

Figure 3 Map of the first phase of the An Lushan Rebellion

Guozhong, whom they blamed for An Lushan's rebellion and the fall of Tong Pass, and labeled him a traitor. Guozhong had unwittingly supplied a pretext for their accusation by appearing to speak conspiratorially with a group of Tibetan envoys in Xuanzong's entourage. The troops killed Guozhong and dismembered his body to vent their fury; one source says they killed the Tibetans too.[51] Next, they forced Xuanzong to order the strangling of Guozhong's cousin Consort Yang (719–56), who had been the emperor's favored concubine and de facto empress since 745. The beautiful consort's death as a scapegoat was romanticized in later Tang literature and has shaped numerous later interpretations of the An Lushan Rebellion as the tragic end of a glamorous age.[52]

Although An Lushan is often caricatured as a boorish barbarian or a duplicitous traitor, he was a strikingly charismatic, complex, and paradoxical figure – reportedly illiterate but conversant in multiple Inner Asian languages; grossly overweight but an excellent military commander and accomplished dancer of the "Sogdian whirl"; kind and generous to his men (many of whom became fiercely loyal to him), but cruel to his foes.[53] In 756, not long into his reign as Emperor of Yan, he began suffering from blurred vision and other physical ailments. This changed his personality and made him reclusive and violently abusive toward his attendants. In early 757, he was murdered by one of these attendants in a conspiracy led by another of his sons, Qingxu (d. 759). The rebellion that he had started continued for another six years: first under Qingxu's ineffectual leadership, then under Lushan's capable Turco-Sogdian general Shi Siming (d. 761), and finally under Siming's son Chaoyi (d. 763).[54] Tang loyalist armies, their ranks bolstered by mass conscription of peasant men, were able to contain the rebel regime to Chang'an, Luoyang, northern Henan, and Hebei. But their cavalry forces were too weak to go on the offensive, so the Tang forged an alliance with the Uighur khaganate on terms of fictive brotherhood and parity (without the usual pretensions of Chinese suzerainty), as well as gifts of silk and promises of plunder. The emperor Suzong (Li Heng, r. 756–62) – who had forced his father Xuanzong into retirement soon after the ignominious retreat from Chang'an – also gave his second daughter (already twice widowed) in

---

[51] *ALS* 104–105; *ZZTJ* 218.6970–74.

[52] Xuanzong did not appoint an empress after deposing Empress Wang in 724. Empress Wang's rival Consort Wu was de facto empress until her death in 737, followed by Consort Yang in 745–55. Consort Yang was originally married to one of Xuanzong's sons in 736–41 but caught Xuanzong's eye and was taken into his harem. She sponsored Yang Guozhong's political rise but was also known to favor An Lushan, even adopting him as a son. Claims that she had an affair with Lushan, however, are highly dubious and did not appear until the eleventh century. See Chen, "Problems of Chinese Historiography."

[53] *ALS* 73–74, 77, 91.

[54] For an accurate and concise narrative of the rebellion, see Graff, *Medieval Chinese Warfare*, 217–23.

marriage to the khagan, an exceptional honor in Tang terms and one clearly conferred out of desperation.

The fearsome Uighur cavalry were crucial to the Tang's ability to retake Chang'an (in 757) and Luoyang (twice, in 757 and 762) but are often criticized in modern historiography for sacking these cities in the process. In fairness, both the Tang and Yan sides, as well as their "barbarian" allies, committed acts of callous brutality and rapacity toward civilians during this war: pillaging cities, murdering prisoners, press-ganging men, robbing and massacring merchants (including foreign merchants), and enslaving women and children.[55] That said, some modern histories that state the death toll from the rebellion as 36 million, nearly two-thirds of the empire's registered population of 52.8 million, are mistaken in overestimating the accuracy of the first post-rebellion census. That census would have been greatly compromised by the loss of local government records and the movement of refugees.[56] There were many imperial subjects still living whom the government was simply unable to register and tax for the time being. A similar situation had existed in the 630s, when the Tang state had only registered 12 million of its subjects compared to the Sui's 46 million in 609.[57] By 839, the Tang empire's registered population had returned to a level of 49.9 million, which would be impossible if only 17 million people survived the violence of 755–63.[58] Claims that the An Lushan Rebellion was the most destructive civil war in world history simply do not hold water.

The An Lushan Rebellion, while ultimately unsuccessful and less devastating than is often claimed, did cause enough disruption to produce lasting changes in the Tang political economy. New military commissionerships were created to fight rebel armies in the interior, or to reward rebel generals who surrendered, until the entire empire was divided into regional commands, each with a sizeable professional army. From this point on, it makes sense to describe the regional commands as provinces and their commissioners as governors. Some provinces, especially in Hebei and Shandong, were effectively autonomous hereditary satrapies, paying no taxes to the imperial court and appointing their own officials. Apart from a period in 782–6, the autonomous governors did not seek to set themselves up as kings or emperors and nominally accepted the Tang dynasty's authority. But their autonomy nonetheless limited the revenue and military resources available to the imperial state, and they were prone to armed resistance when the state attempted to reassert direct rule.[59]

---

[55] Yang, "Letting the Troops Loose," 40–46.
[56] This misconception was popularized by Pinker, *The Better Angels of Our Nature*, Chapter 5. For the Tang's registered population in 755 and 765, see *ZZTJ* 217.6929, 223.7171.
[57] Graff, *Medieval Chinese Warfare*, 183.   [58] *ZZTJ* 246.7942.
[59] Graff, *Medieval Chinese Warfare*, 228–39.

In 758, the imperial state responded to the loss of revenue from the rebels' occupation of agriculturally rich Hebei by introducing a monopoly on the production and sale of an essential commodity, salt. This was effectively an indirect tax on consumers, collected through licensed salt merchants who would buy salt from the state at marked-up prices and pass on the extra cost to their customers. In the long run, income from the salt monopoly made up for that lost from the autonomous provinces and became a pillar of the central government's fiscal health. In addition, a tax reform in 780 shifted a larger proportion of the tax burden from ordinary peasant households to landlord and merchant families outside the tax-exempt official class. As a result of these changes, the state became less inclined to enforce its formerly stringent restrictions on commercial activity and private land ownership, leading to a growing concentration of wealth in the hands of merchant and landlord families, as well as increased commerce in major cities. During the rebellion years, refugees headed south to escape from the fighting, and the resulting population growth drove commercialization and urbanization in the Huainan and Jiangnan (lower Yangzi) regions, where the salt industry was also centered. Interregional commerce flourished, facilitated by waterborne transportation via the Grand Canal and other canals and rivers in the south. The Chinese empire's economic and demographic center shifted permanently from the North China Plain to Jiangnan, which had already once developed into a center of culture and commerce during the centuries of north–south division but had been deliberately peripheralized under the Sui and early Tang.[60]

Commercialization in south China in turn fueled an expansion of maritime trade with the Indian Ocean world – especially in Chinese ceramic wares, which became extremely popular in Abbasid Iraq in the late eighth and ninth centuries and were well suited to transportation in large quantities by sea.[61] The Belitung wreck, an Arab or Indian merchant ship that sank near Srivijaya (a Malay trading thalassocracy based in Sumatra) circa 830, contained some 60,000 ceramic bowls mass-produced in south Chinese kilns and packed tightly in large stone jars, as well as a small number of exquisite gold and silver vessels that may have been a gift from the Tang court to a foreign ruler.[62] Indian Ocean trade routes between the Middle East, South and Southeast Asia, and China continued to prosper through the next five centuries, sustaining large expatriate merchant communities of Arabs and Iranians in south Chinese port cities and

---

[60] Ibid., 239–41; Von Glahn, *The Economic History of China*, 208–17. On the pre-Sui political economy of Jiangnan, see Chittick, *The Jiankang Empire.*
[61] George, "Direct Sea Trade," 604–605.
[62] Heng, "An Ordinary Ship"; Heng, "The Tang Shipwreck."

eventually also facilitating the spread of Islam to insular Southeast Asia.[63] Chinese participation in maritime commerce remained passive in late Tang times, however, due to both legal restrictions and technological limitations. Chinese merchants only began sailing to Southeast Asia and the Indian Ocean in large numbers in the late tenth and eleventh centuries, encouraged by the Song dynasty's (960–1276) liberalization of laws on maritime trade, as well as advances in Chinese shipbuilding and the invention of the maritime compass.[64]

While indirectly benefiting the south Chinese economy and Indian Ocean trade, the An Lushan Rebellion also started a chain of events that amounted to a gradual but irreversible collapse of the Tang empire's western frontiers. In early 756, the Tang court ordered the Shuofang (Ordos), Hexi (Gansu Corridor), and Longyou (Qinghai front) commands to deploy their best troops to Tong Pass. Most of these units were destroyed in Qoshu Han's defeat; more troops were then mobilized from these commands, as well as Anxi, to form the core of a new Tang loyalist army. The Tibetans used the resulting hollowing-out of the Longyou army to capture Shibaocheng and other forts on the Qinghai front.[65] The rest of the Longyou command had fallen by the end of 760. The Tibetans moved on to take much of southern Gansu in 761–2, putting their armies within striking range of Chang'an. At this point, the Tangut and Qiang *jimi* polities of the Longyou frontier realigned themselves with the Tibetans and began raiding the Chang'an region.[66] Some Tang prefectures in mountainous northwestern Sichuan also fell, while the Yunnan kingdom of Nanzhao seized all Tang prefectures and garrisons south of the Dadu River and thus gained a northern border nearly invulnerable to attack.[67] The king of Nanzhao had rebelled against Tang suzerainty in 750 and transferred his allegiance to the Tibetan *tsenpo* (emperor), who conferred on him the title *tsenpo chung* (younger brother of the *tsenpo*).[68] In 751–4, Xuanzong (on the urging of Yang Guozhong) had launched two massive punitive expeditions against Nanzhao using Tang troops based in Sichuan; both failed with heavy losses.[69] Now the tables were turned, and the Tibetans could call on their Yunnanese vassals to supply manpower for attacks on the Tang in Sichuan.

---

[63] Wade, "An Early Age of Commerce"; Wade, "Islam Across the Indian Ocean"; Chaffee, *The Muslim Merchants of Premodern China*.

[64] For more on this subject, see Heng, *Southeast Asian Interactions*.

[65] *ZZTJ* 217.6938, 6943, 218.6981, 6987, 219.7011, 7018, 220.7038, 221.7096; *JTS* 196a.5236; *XTS* 216b.6087.

[66] *ZZTJ* 220.7060, 221.7090, 7092, 7100, 7102, 222.7105, 223.7146.

[67] *ZZTJ* 218.7000, 223.7158–59; *JTS* 196a.5237.

[68] Bryson, "Tsenpo Chung, Yunnan Wang, Mahārāja."

[69] Backus, *The Nan-chao Kingdom*, 40–77.

Only in the mountains of Guangxi was the Tang military able to hold the line. In 756, after troops from the Lingnan regional command (encompassing Guangdong and Guangxi) were diverted to the north to fight the rebels, a coalition of Lao chiefs began attacking Tang prefectures in the region. At its height, the rebellion is said to have mobilized some 200,000 Lao and included at least eight chiefs who assumed the title "king." In 759, Suzong successfully used an offer of amnesty to undermine the rebel coalition, peeling away a rival faction of chiefs and using it to attack and kill seven of the Lao kings. Suzong then pardoned all other rebels who surrendered and even rewarded them with gifts of silk.[70] Suzong's conciliatory approach to the Lao revolt was a stark contrast to Xuanzong's policy of ruthlessly exterminating southern "barbarian" rebels, or at least attempting to do so in the case of Nanzhao.[71] This was less a reflection of greater humaneness than of the dearth of military resources that the Tang empire faced while struggling to contain the An Lushan Rebellion.

At some point during his reign, Suzong even began paying tribute in silk to the Tibetan *tsenpo* Trisong Detsen (r. 755–97). This act of appeasement, presumably meant to obviate incursions from the west while the Tang concentrated on defeating the rebels, may well have been an outcome of the Tang–Tibetan peace covenant agreed upon in early 762.[72] Chinese sources are silent on the covenant's terms, but we can deduce them from the *Old Tibetan Annals*, as well as a commemorative inscription erected by the Tibetan general and minister Takdra Lukhong in 764. Both Tibetan texts state that after Suzong's death in May 762, his successor Daizong (Li Yu, r. 762–79) refused to continue paying tribute to Tibet, finding this "unsuitable" or "improper."[73] The extent of Daizong's efforts to restore the "proper" hierarchy in Tang–Tibetan relations can be seen from Tang records, which falsely claim that in mid-762, Tibetan envoys arrived in Chang'an to present a tribute of local products to him![74]

Trisong Detsen responded to Daizong's attempt at reasserting Chinese superiority by launching a punitive attack on the Tang capital itself. In the winter of 763, a massive expeditionary army of 200,000 Tibetans, *Tuygun (Tuyuhun), Tanguts, and Qiang, commanded by Takdra Lukhong, drove deep into Tang territory from Gansu. Daizong's court, caught off guard, was forced to abandon Chang'an and flee eastwards. The Tibetan expedition entered Chang'an, installed a captured imperial clansman as the new emperor, and pillaged the

---

[70] *JTS* 157.4143–44; *XTS* 222c.6330. On the Lao peoples, see Yang, *Early Tang China and the World*, Section 7.

[71] Yang, "Letting the Troops Loose," 32–33.

[72] *ZZTJ* 222.7118; *CFYG* 981.11360; *JTS* 196a.5237; Lin, *Yubo gange*, 388–90.

[73] The inscription states the size of the tribute as 50,000 bolts of silk annually. For translations of these texts, see Dotson, *The Old Tibetan Annals*, 132, 148–49.

[74] *JTS* 196a.5237; *CFYG* 972.11248.

city before departing.[75] Daizong soon returned to Chang'an and removed the Tibetans' puppet government, but more Tibetan attacks on the Tang capital region (again including Tuygun, Tangut, and Qiang contingents) came in 764 and 765. These assaults were even more threatening than the first, as they were coordinated with attacks by the Uighurs and the renegade Shuofang governor Buqut (Pugu) Huai'en (d. 765), who controlled the Ordos region.

Buqut Huai'en, like An Lushan, was essentially pushed into rebelling by enemies in the imperial bureaucracy.[76] Hailing from a lineage of eastern Tegreg *jimi* chiefs, he had served with distinction as a general in the Shuofang army both before and during the An Lushan Rebellion. Huai'en had also helped to broker the crucial military alliance with the Uighurs, marrying one of his daughters to the Uighur khagan's son in the process. Yet after the rebellion ended, Huai'en's ties to the Uighur khagan laid him open to accusations of disloyalty, even though Suzong himself had arranged the marriage. Daizong increasingly believed Huai'en's accusers, forcing him to revolt out of anger and desperation. In 764, he invited the Tibetans and Uighurs to join him in a raid on Chang'an, which failed due to an unexpectedly well-prepared Tang defense under the veteran general Guo Ziyi (697–781) and an attack on his rear by Tang forces from the Gansu Corridor. Huai'en initiated a second joint raid on Chang'an in 765, only to die of a sudden illness en route. Guo Ziyi then met with the Uighur contingent at Jingyang, some 20 miles north of Chang'an, and convinced it to turn on the Tibetans. The Tibetan contingent fled, suffering heavy losses at the hands of pursuing Uighur and Tang cavalry. Most accounts of Guo's feat, concerned with accentuating his heroism and preserving Chinese dignity, attribute it to the Uighurs' respect for his renowned prowess on the battlefield during the An Lushan Rebellion. But other evidence suggests that Guo effectively bribed them into changing sides. He had brought 3,000 bolts of varicolored silk to the negotiations, and Daizong personally presented 100,000 more bolts of silk to the Uighur contingent after the Tibetans retreated. The Tang court had to empty its treasury (already looted by the Tibetans in 763) and cut its officials' salary to afford such a lavish reward.[77]

The Tang thus weathered the crisis of Buqut Huai'en's revolt, but wealth in silk was not the only price it paid in the long run: In 764, the Hexi command had sacrificed its best troops in the attack on Shuofang that forced Huai'en to abort

---

[75] *ZZTJ* 223.7150–54; Dotson, *The Old Tibetan Annals*, 132, 147–49. The Tuygun khaganate had become a vassal state of the Tibetan empire in 663, following nearly thirty years of alignment with the Tang: see Yang, *Early Tang China and the World*, Sections 3 and 4.

[76] The best English-language study of Huai'en's revolt remains Peterson, "P'u-ku Huai'en and the T'ang Court."

[77] *ZZTJ* 223.7180–84.

his raid on Chang'an. Consequently, the Hexi headquarters at Liangzhou (Wuwei, Gansu) fell to a Tibetan attack effectively cutting off Tang prefectures and garrisons in the Gansu Corridor and Central Asia from the rest of the empire (Figure 4).[78] Preoccupied with fending off the pillaging and slaving raids that the Tibetans mounted into Shaanxi, Ningxia, and Sichuan nearly every autumn, the Tang could not mount a counteroffensive to reconquer Gansu. The isolated garrisons on the old northwestern frontier maintained intermittent contact with the Tang court through the Uighurs, but the Tibetans overwhelmed them one by one over the next twenty-five years. In 784, Emperor Dezong (Li Kuo, r. 779–805) even pledged to cede the Tarim and Dzungarian Basins to the Tibetan empire in exchange for military aid against another rebellion that had driven him out of Chang'an.[79] Trisong Detsen did send an army against the rebels, but Dezong later reneged on his promise after his ministers criticized it as strategically unwise.[80] This made little difference to the outcome, since the beleaguered Tang garrisons in Central Asia could not hold out forever even with military support from the Uighurs. By circa 800, nearly all had fallen into Tibetan hands except for Beshbalik, which the Uighurs now controlled (Figure 5). The Uighurs then began to war with the Tibetans over Turfan (Xizhou/Gaochang) and the Tarim Basin.[81] The details of this struggle remain very difficult to reconstruct due to limited sources, but it is likely that the Uighurs had taken Turfan, Agni, and Kucha from the Tibetans by the 820s.

4 An Anti-foreign (or Anti-Sogdian) Backlash?

Some historians have read Buqut Huai'en's fate as evidence that the Tang court became distrustful of its ethnically "foreign" (*Fan*) generals after An Lushan's rebellion.[82] Others have argued that An Lushan's Turco-Sogdian ethnicity triggered a violent anti-Sogdian backlash among the Tang elite, forcing Sogdians in the empire to conceal their ethnic origins by claiming Chinese ancestry.[83] These theories are based on flawed and oversimplistic readings of historical evidence. They are also predicated on an influential but equally flawed grand narrative that, as I noted earlier, reads the An Lushan Rebellion and the Tang's consequent loss of its Central Asian empire as a turning point in

---

[78] *ZZTJ* 223.7168–69.
[79] This rebellion began in late 783 as a mutiny of disgruntled troops in Chang'an but quickly escalated when Dezong fled the capital and the general whom the mutineers had chosen as their leader declared himself an emperor. The rebel regime failed to capture Dezong and crumbled under a loyalist counterattack in mid-784.
[80] *ZZTJ* 229.7399, 230.7403, 7422, 231.7429, 7442.   [81] *ZZTJ* 233.7520–22, 234.7552.
[82] For example, Fu, *Han Tang shilun ji*, 214–18.
[83] Most prominently Rong, *Zhonggu Zhongguo yu Sute wenming*, 79–113.

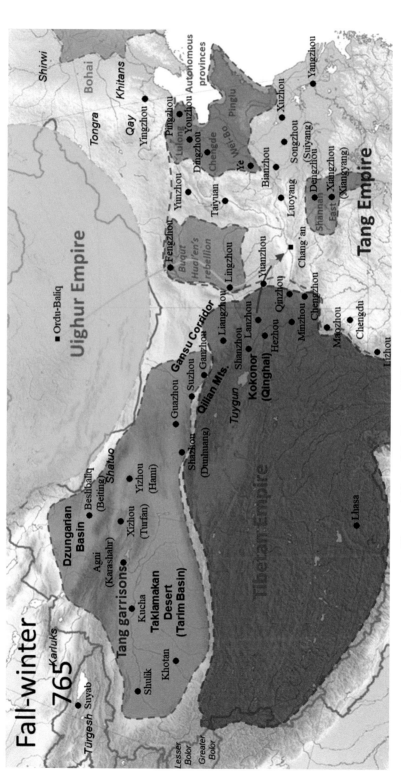

Figure 4 Map of the Tang and Tibetan empires in 765

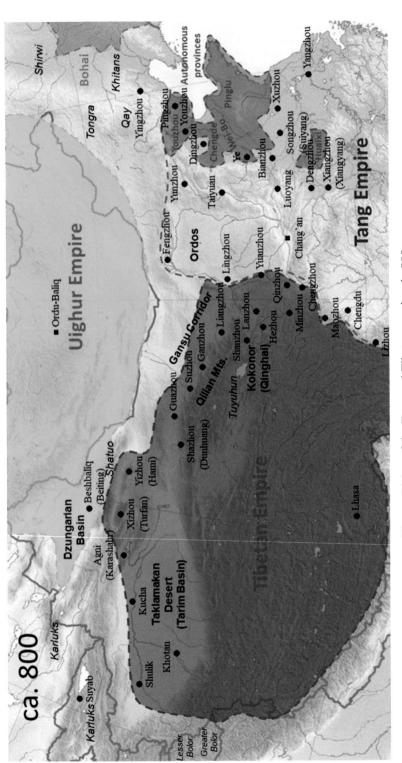

Figure 5 Map of the Tang and Tibetan empires in 800

Chinese attitudes toward foreign peoples and cultures, which supposedly changed from "cosmopolitan" to xenophobic.[84]

The notion that the Tang court became distrustful of ethnically non-Chinese generals after An Lushan rebelled can be quite easily refuted. Both the Tang and rebel sides were highly multiethnic. The rebel army included commanders and soldiers of Khitan, *Qay (Xi), Goguryeo, Turco-Sogdian, and Eastern Türk origin, drawn from the Fanyang and Pinglu commands, as well as allied contingents of Tongra (Tongluo), Qay, Khitans, and *Shirwi (Shiwei) from eastern Inner Mongolia. Lushan was said to have a personal bodyguard of more than 8,000 Tongra, Qay and Khitan warriors, many of them captives taken in punitive raids; they were fiercely loyal to him as he had adopted them as sons and paid them handsomely.[85] But the Tang defense of Chang'an in 756 was entrusted to the equally "non-Chinese" Qoshu Han, and Qoshu's army at Tong Pass included contingents of Tegreg, Tuygun, and Qiang levied from the northwestern *jimi* polities.[86] After Qoshu was captured by the rebels, the Tang side's ablest remaining generals included the Khitan Li Guangbi (708–64), the Goguryeoan Wang Sili (d. 761), and the Kuchean Bai Xiaode (714–79), as well as the Tegreg Buqut Huai'en and the ethnically Chinese Guo Ziyi. While the Tang turned to the Uighurs for aid, contingents of troops from at least ten Central Asian states, including Fergana, Khotan, and Tokharistan, also came to fight the rebels at the summons of the Tang court, usually accompanying reinforcements from the Anxi Protectorate. The Khotanese contingent of 5,000 men was led by the king of Khotan himself, who handed his throne over to his brother and remained in Chang'an afterward, living in considerable luxury.[87] In 757, the recapture of Chang'an even featured a mysterious contingent of Arabs, who may have been mercenaries or former rebels against the Abbasids.[88] In short, the An Lushan Rebellion was hardly a simple clash between Chinese on one side and "barbarians" on the other.[89]

The Tang court did become more suspicious of powerful and popular generals after the An Lushan Rebellion, but this problem affected commanders of both Chinese and non-Chinese ethnicity, including both Guo Ziyi and Li Guangbi. Proud, strong-willed characters like Guangbi and Buqut Huai'en (who, it should be noted, did not work well together) tended to fall afoul of the court bureaucracy after rising to eminence. But the case of the Tegreg general *Qun Jian (Hun Jian, 736–800) suggests that this had much more to do with personality than with ethnicity. Qun Jian rendered sterling service to the

---

[84] See Yang, *The Way of the Barbarians*, 3–7.
[85] *ALS* 82. The Tongra were an eastern Tegreg people, while the Qay and Shirwi were Mongolic speakers related culturally to the Khitan and Serbi.
[86] *ALS* 97.   [87] *ZZTJ* 218.6998, 219.7010, 7014; *XTS* 110.4127–28.
[88] Inaba, "Arab Soldiers in Tang China."   [89] See also Skaff, "Barbarians at the Gates?"

Tang against Tibetan and rebel armies from the 760s to the 780s and was rewarded with a princedom and a rank equivalent to chief minister. His case was not an outlier: Numerous generals of Turkic or other Inner Asian origin are known to have played prominent roles in the late Tang military, both in autonomous provinces and in provinces under direct imperial authority. Like Huai'en, Qun Jian was from a *jimi* chief lineage and had started his career as an officer in the Shuofang army, accompanying his father (also a Shuofang officer) on tours of duty from the age of ten. His official biographies make it clear that he consistently took care to display humble and deferential behavior toward the imperial court and thus retained Dezong's trust and favor throughout his career.[90] In contrast, his equally accomplished, ethnically Chinese, but less circumspect colleague Li Sheng (727–93) was eventually stripped of his command in 787 after Dezong believed calumnious accusations sown by the Tibetans and Li's political enemies. Li was known for openly contradicting Dezong on matters of foreign policy and displaying contempt for colleagues whom he found lacking in moral integrity.[91]

Some proponents of the theory of a specifically anti-Sogdian backlash have cited a massacre of Sogdians said to have occurred in Youzhou in early 761.[92] They identify the massacre's perpetrators as Tang imperial troops retaking the city, but this misreads the evidence, as Youzhou was still in rebel hands until early 763. There are three surviving eighth-century accounts of the massacre, but they all clearly state that the Youzhou massacre happened during a phase of internecine conflict and anarchy among the rebels after Shi Chaoyi seized power from his father Siming in a coup. Both rebel factions appear to have used non-Chinese troops in their battles for control over Youzhou, but the rebel general Gao Juren's troops were primarily of Chinese and possibly Goguryeo descent, while his rivals Ashina Chengqing and Kang Xiaozhong rallied Turkic and Sogdian (or Turco-Sogdian) troops to their side.[93] Chengqing and Xiaozhong were defeated and driven out of the city, but Juren suspected the Sogdians remaining in the city of being on their side. Two of our sources – the *Biography of An Lushan* (*An Lushan shiji*) and the *Account of the Disorder in Youzhou* (*Jimen jiluan*) – contain nearly the exact same narrative of what happened next, with only minor differences in wording:

> Juren ordered the city's residents to kill Sogdians [*Hu*] in exchange for big rewards. As a result, the *Kjet-Sogdians [*Jie Hu*] were wiped out. Even their

---

[90] *JTS* 134.3703–10; *XTS* 155.4891–4894.   [91] *JTS* 133.3674; *XTS* 154.4863–72.

[92] For example, Vaissière, *Sogdian Traders*, 220.

[93] Ashina Chengqing's surname indicates descent from the Eastern Türk aristocracy. Kang Xiaozhong's surname was frequently used by Sogdians in China to indicate origin from Samarkand. Gao Juren's surname was used by the aristocracy of Goguryeo, but also found among the Chinese.

small children were thrown into the air and impaled on spears. Very many [non-Sogdians] were wrongfully killed because they had high noses and looked like Sogdians.[94]

Another, significantly different account is found in the *Annals of Henan* (*Heluo chunqiu*). It claims that "Prince Ashina" executed Gao Juren (here called Jiuren) but was then defeated and driven from Youzhou by another general, Gao Ruzhen. Shi Chaoyi then summoned Ashina to Luoyang and massacred every "*Hu*-faced" (i.e., high-nosed) person in his army.[95] This would have been a rather bizarre act given that Shi Chaoyi himself was most likely Turco-Sogdian. Whatever the case, every extant source on these events places them in the context of internal conflict among the rebels, not anti-Sogdian prejudice on the part of the Tang court.

The extent to which Sogdian identity or solidarity played a role in An Lushan's rebellion remains open to question.[96] According to the *Biography of An Lushan*, which served as the basic source for all later biographies of its subject, Lushan was born to an Eastern Türk shamaness, who conceived him miraculously after praying to the Turkic god of war, *Yaluoshan* (after whom she named the child). She later married a Turco-Sogdian soldier named An Yanyan or An Yiyan, who thus became Lushan's stepfather. Lushan and his cousin Sishun grew up in the Eastern Türk khaganate and migrated to the Tang as refugees in the mid-710s, first arriving in northern Shanxi and then settling in Yingzhou, which the Tang had reoccupied in 717.[97] The *Biography* also claims that for eight to nine years before 755, Lushan colluded with Sogdian merchants throughout the empire to procure funds and materials with which to found a rebel regime:

He secretly used Sogdian merchants to trade in the various circuits [of the empire], and they brought in millions of prized goods from other regions every year. Whenever the merchants arrived, Lushan would dress in Sogdian

---

[94] *ALS* 112; *ZZTJ* 222.7110. The author of this narrative seems to have drawn inspiration from an early seventh-century account of the massacre of the *Kjet (Jie 羯) population of Ye (Linzhang, Hebei) in 349, during the collapse of the Kjet-ruled Later Zhao state. The Kjet were associated with the Xiongnu but had facial features similar to the Sogdians and other Central Asians: deep-set eyes, high noses, and full beards. As a result of this similarity, Tang propaganda against An Lushan frequently denigrated him as a Kjet or a Kjet-Sogdian (Jie-Hu) to accentuate his "barbarian" origin. See Fang *et al.*, *Jinshu*, 107.2791–92; Huang, "'Jie-Hu,' 'Zhejie,' 'Zazhong Hu' kaobian."

[95] The eleventh-century *Xin Tangshu* largely follows this version while changing "Prince Ashina" 阿史那王 to the name "Ashina Yu" 阿史那玉, most likely a transcriber's error. *ZZTJ* 222.7111–12; *XTS* 225a.6432.

[96] One influential scholar takes such solidarity as given: "The Sogdians of Turfan, the *sabao* of Gansu, the Sogdian horse breeders of the Ordos, the small and great merchants of the capital as well as the great generals all knew that they belonged to a shared community, that of the *hu* of North China." Vaissière, *Sogdian Traders*, 219 (on *sabao*, a title held many Sogdian community leaders in China, see 148–52).

[97] *ALS* 73.

clothing and sit on a couch, with incense burning and treasures laid out for display. He would have a hundred Sogdians in attendance at his side and another crowd of Sogdians prostrating themselves in a ring around him, praying for blessings from Heaven. Lushan would have many sacrificial animals led out, and shamans would beat drums and sing and dance until the gathering ended at dusk. He then ordered the Sogdians to buy silk secretly in the various circuits, which he used to manufacture millions of robes of red and violet silk, gold and silver fish-shaped pouches, and belts [i.e., attire for court officials].[98]

Some modern historians have used this passage as evidence for a sense of ethnic solidarity between Sogdian merchants from Central Asia and Turco-Sogdian soldiers like An Lushan, founded on their common Zoroastrian religion. This is not implausible, but there is also a strong likelihood that this part of the *Biography* account is apocryphal, constructed for the sake of accentuating Lushan's cultural otherness or barbarism and the illegitimacy of his bid for rulership over the Chinese civilization-state, regardless of his superficial adoption of its sartorial trappings. Modern scholars have long rejected the *Biography* explanation for the origins of Lushan's name, instead interpreting it as the Sogdian name *Roxšan* (*Rokhshan*), meaning "bright."[99] This should alert us to the fact that the *Biography* cannot be read uncritically as evidence of Lushan's cultural and religious identity or its relevance to his revolt. As noted earlier, the very idea that Lushan planned and prepared for his rebellion years in advance is questionable.

The evidence for Sogdian merchants being sympathizers with An Lushan's rebellion is very thin. In early 757, a Chinese military officer named Ge Tinglun and a Sogdian merchant named An Menwu led a revolt at Liangzhou, killed the Hexi military commissioner Zhou Bi, and seized control of much of the prefecture. The rebels are said to have numbered 60,000 and are generically labeled *Hu*, but they probably included Sogdians, Tegreg, and Chinese soldiers and civilians.[100] Liangzhou had a large, centuries-old community of immigrant Sogdians, but the sources give no indication that their motivation for rebelling was ethnic affinity to An Lushan. It is equally possible that the revolt arose from local conditions at Liangzhou, including the destabilizing effect of deploying large numbers of Hexi troops eastward to fight the rebels. Indeed, one source states that the "*Hu* tribes" of Hexi (the Gansu Corridor) had already descended into a state of civil war since the summer of 756, as their chiefs had led troop contingents to help defend Tong Pass and were believed to have been killed or

---

[98] *ALS* 83; compare. Vaissière, *Sogdian Traders*, 218, which contains some mistranslations.
[99] This etymology was first proposed to Edwin Pulleyblank by the Iranologist Walter B. Henning: Pulleyblank, "The Background and Early Life of An Lu-shan," 22–23.
[100] *ZZTJ* 219.7015.

captured during Qoshu Han's defeat. These tribes were most likely Tegreg, not Sogdian, and we are told that rival contenders for tribal leadership began to fight one another. Xuanzong then appointed Zhou Bi to pacify the unrest as the new Hexi military commissioner.[101] Zhou, a senior officer in the Hexi army who had survived the Tong Pass disaster, apparently failed in this task, leading his Chinese colleague to overthrow him with the help of the Sogdian community. However, loyalist troops in the prefectural garrison regrouped and crushed the rebellion after seventeen days.

Some historians have also pointed to a contemporaneous revolt by the Turco-Sogdian population of the Ordos region, the so-called "Sogdians (*Hu*) of the Six Prefectures," as evidence for Sogdians rallying to An Lushan's banner.[102] These Ordos rebels were descended from Turco-Sogdians who had been captured and resettled with the Eastern Türks in 630. In 679, the Tang court moved them to the southwestern Ordos, divided them into six new prefectures, and placed them under the authority of Chinese prefects to prevent them from joining the Eastern Türk revolt. In 721–2 this population rose in rebellion, possibly because the Tang court had recently ruled that they must pay taxes in grain, cloth, and corvée labor like regular Tang subjects, rather than the lighter *jimi*-style tax in sheep that they had previously paid.[103] The Tang government suppressed the rebels and dispersed some 50,000 of them in Henan to prevent further unrest, but moved them back to a new prefecture in the Ordos in 738.[104] In mid-756, shortly after the fall of Chang'an, some 5,000 Tongra and Eastern Türk auxiliary cavalry in the rebel army left and attempted to found an independent state in the Ordos. The leader of this effort, it should be noted, was not a Sogdian but an Eastern Türk aristocrat, Ashina Congli; the sources disagree over whether he was acting on his own or under An Lushan's orders. Within a few months, Congli had rallied tens of thousands of Turco-Sogdians to his banner. Tang and Uighur forces defeated Congli in the winter of 756–7, killing 30,000 of his followers and capturing another 10,000, but some Turco-Sogdian survivors must have fled to rebel-held Luoyang, as Tongra and "Sogdians of the Six Prefectures" were supposedly among the rebel forces that retreated into Hebei after a Tang–Uighur counteroffensive recaptured Luoyang in 757.[105] Other

---

[101] The post of Hexi military commissioner had previously been held by Qoshu Han, who was jointly military commissioner of Longyou. *ZZTJ* 218.6979.

[102] Vaissière, *Sogdian Traders*, 218.

[103] Iwami, "Turks and Sogdians," 43–47, 57–59, 62–64; Yang, *Frontiers of the Tang and Song Empires*, Map 6, 6d, at https://storymaps.arcgis.com/stories/0cf798878745406fa5719b97ccf c5454#ref-n-Ar2rKw; Yang, "Letting the Troops Loose," 30–32.

[104] *ZZTJ* 212.6752, 214.6832; Yang, *Frontiers of the Tang and Song Empires*, Map 6, 6e, at https://storymaps.arcgis.com/stories/0cf798878745406fa5719b97ccfc5454#ref-n-Ar2rKw.

[105] *ZZTJ* 218.6986, 6997–98, 219.7007, 220.7047.

Turco-Sogdians stayed in the Ordos until 786, when the Tang moved them to northern Shanxi to prevent them from collaborating with raiding Tibetan armies.[106] It appears, then, that the Ordos Turco-Sogdians joined hands with Ashina Congli not because of ethnic affinity to An Lushan but because of resentment at being controlled by the Tang state. They would have welcomed any external help with breaking free of such control, regardless of the ethnicity of its source.

Evidence of anti-Sogdian animus at the Tang court in the aftermath of An Lushan's revolt is surprisingly lacking. Most of the Tang elite simply does not seem to have believed in what we would call ethnic profiling. Guilt by association was built into the legal system, but it was based on familial ties and patronage networks, not ethnic category. The Tang court was certainly not above publicly denigrating An Lushan or Shi Siming as "renegade Sogdians" (*ni Hu*) to delegitimate their claims to the Mandate of Heaven, but it knew better than to let political rhetoric dictate actual policy. It is true that early in the rebellion, An Sishun was removed from his position as Shuofang military commissioner and replaced with Guo Ziyi to avoid conflicts of interest. But no other Sogdian in the Tang army is known to have received similar treatment. Even in Sishun's case, Xuanzong retained him as minister of revenue and only executed him after Qoshu Han (who detested both Sishun and Lushan) used a forged letter to accuse him of conspiring with Lushan.[107] A Sogdian general unrelated to Lushan, An Baoyu (formerly named An Chongzhang, 704–77), did request and receive permission in 757 to adopt the imperial surname Li (an honor typically conferred on meritorious generals of any ethnicity) so as to remove any hint of association with Lushan. In 762, he further obtained Daizong's permission for his whole clan to use the surname Li and change its official ancestral home from Liangzhou to Chang'an. Baoyu and his younger cousin Baozhen (733–94) served with loyalty and distinction throughout the rebellions of An Lushan and Buqut Huai'en, rising to the highest ranks of the military and civil bureaucracies and never once facing suspicion over their Sogdian heritage.[108] But this can hardly have been due only to a surname change, since their official biographies make no effort to conceal their An ancestry.[109]

Contrary to Antonino Forte's claim that from the time An Lushan rebelled, "anyone with the family name An was suspected of being a rebel or a criminal,"

---

[106] *ZZTJ* 232.7477.
[107] *ZZTJ* 217.6937, 217.6957. Sishun's younger brother Yuanzhen was at first appointed to fill the post previously held by the unfortunate An Qingzong. Yuanzhen was later executed together with Sishun; other members of both their families were exiled to the far south.
[108] *JTS* 132.3645–50; *XTS* 138.4619–23.　　　[109] *Contra* Vaissière, *Sogdian Traders*, 221.

it would in fact have been absurd to associate Baoyu with Lushan simply because of their surname, which all Sogdians with ancestral origins from Bukhara (known to the Chinese as the state of An) tended to use in China.[110] Despite their shared Chinese surname, Lushan and Baoyu were not kinsmen, and their backgrounds were entirely different.[111] Baoyu's ancestors had settled in Liangzhou in the sixth century, and his great-great-grandfather An Xinggui was recognized as a major contributor to the rise of the Tang, having coordinated a pro-Tang revolt by the Liangzhou Sogdians that overthrew the local warlord of Gansu.[112] One of Xinggui's sons, An Yuanshou (606–83), served as Taizong's bodyguard in 626–7, participated in the Xuanwu Gate Coup, and was a military commander in Gaozong's campaigns against the Western Türks in the 650s.[113] While Baoyu and Baozhen followed a military career path, other branches of their clan are said to have moved to Chang'an, acquired a classical education, and intermarried with literati families.[114] Moreover, the epitaph of Baoyu's father An Zhongjing (661–726) shows that by the early eighth century, the An clan had begun elevating its prestige by claiming descent from the mythical Sinitic sage-king Huangdi through one of his grandsons, who supposedly went to Iran and founded the kingdom of Anxi (the Han Chinese name for Arsacid Parthia). Instead of Sogdian immigrants, they now traced their roots in China to An Shigao, a Parthian prince said to have come to the Han empire as a Buddhist missionary in 148 CE. Baoyu and his descendants maintained this fictive genealogy even after changing their surname to Li.[115] To our knowledge, the Turco-Sogdian An Lushan never made such claims to either Sinitic or Parthian descent; they would have meant little to him, given his lack of Sinitic classical and historical education. In short, the An clan of Liangzhou had, over several generations, developed strong social and cultural connections among the Tang elite, while most likely losing much of its attachment to its Sogdian heritage. Members of the clan had no reason to feel any affinity to new Turco-Sogdian immigrants like An Lushan. The Tang court understood that the empire's Sogdian subjects were not a monolithic group but

---

[110] Forte, "Iranians in China," 279.

[111] *Pace* Forte, who suggested in 1995 that Baoyu and Lushan might have been distantly related via adoption but provided no solid evidence for it. Forte, *The Hostage An Shigao*, 101–102.

[112] *JTS* 55.2251–52; *ZZTJ* 187.5855.

[113] Yuanshou's life is known from his epitaph, unearthed in 1972. Niu, "An Yuanshou muzhiming."

[114] *JTS* 132.3645.

[115] The claim to descent from Huangdi and An Shigao is also found in the official An clan genealogy at *XTS* 75b.3445–48. I agree with Kuwabara Jitsuzō and Étienne de la Vaissière that the clan's claim of An Shigao as an ancestor is probably as fictitious as its claim of descent from Huangdi, *pace* Forte who took it as factual and strenuously rejected the idea that the An of Liangzhou originated from Bukhara. Vaissière, *Sogdian Traders*, 62–63; Forte, *The Hostage An Shigao*; Forte, "Kuwabara's Misleading Thesis."

rather multiple diasporic communities with different histories; unfortunately, modern scholarship has not always shared this awareness.

It has been argued that most Sogdian families in China, save "families whose records of service were beyond suspicion," began claiming Chinese ancestry to avoid persecution after the An Lushan Rebellion, resulting in assimilation into the Chinese population within a few generations.[116] Such arguments are founded on a number of late Tang epitaphs that appear to ascribe an ancestral home (also known as a native place or choronym) in south China to a Sogdian subject. But the identification of some of these subjects as Sogdian has been challenged, since some surnames used by Sogdian families were also common among the Chinese (e.g., He, Cao, Kang, Shǐ 史, and Shí 石).[117] This issue exposes a logical flaw in the theory: It would have been much more practical and effective for Sogdians to conceal their ethnicity by changing to a Chinese surname that wasn't among the six or seven commonly used by Sogdians in China to denote their state of origin (e.g., An for Bukhara, Kang for Samarkand, and Shí for Chach). Some historians have claimed that surname changes were an option only to those with good political connections.[118] But that was the case only with adopting the prestigious imperial surname Li. A Kang could become a Wang or Zhang even if he couldn't become a Li, and if he did, his Sogdian ancestry would be totally invisible in his epitaph, though his facial features could still give it away while he was living.

If some Sogdian families retained their surnames but began claiming a south Chinese ancestral home on their epitaphs during the late Tang period, the most likely reason is not fear of persecution but social climbing, similar to the case of the Liangzhou An clan claiming the prestige of descent from Huangdi and Parthian royalty. Consider the Sogdian Kang clan of Lingzhou, which produced four generations of Tang generals. These included Kang Zhi, who made his name by capturing the Ordos Turco-Sogdian rebel leader Kang Daibin in 721, and Kang Zhi's grandson Kang Rizhi (d. 789), who was ennobled as Prince of Guiji Commandery in circa 785. Kang Zhi and his sons identified Lingzhou, rather than Samarkand in Sogdiana, as their ancestral home. Starting from Rizhi's generation, however, members of the Kang clan claimed Guiji (Shaoxing, Zhejiang) in the south, not Lingzhou in the northwest, as their native place in epitaphs. On one level, this was linked to the prestige of Rizhi's noble title. But some recent research suggests that Rizhi requested a fief in Guiji from the Tang court because of the social prestige of association with another Kang

---

[116] Vaissière, *Sogdian Traders*, 221–22. For a similar opinion, see Rong, *Zhonggu Zhongguo yu Sute wenming*, 86–99.

[117] Wang, *Tangdai Suteren Huahua wenti*, 65–72.

[118] Vaissière, *Sogdian Traders*, 221; Rong, *Zhonggu Zhongguo yu Sute wenming*, 88.

lineage of Chinese literati officials that had recently risen to prominence there.[119] If, in the 780s, Kang Rizhi was being persecuted for his Sogdian origins, he could hardly have obtained permission from the court to associate his family with Guiji. In fact, he would not have been given a noble title and a fief at all.

It was once thought that an anti-Sogdian backlash in Chang'an drove Sogdian families to migrate to the autonomous provinces of Hebei, which were supposedly more tolerant due to the multiethnic origins of their military governors. Recent research shows this to be untrue. There were certainly a good number of Sogdians in Hebei, some of whom became military commissioners, but there were also probably more Sogdians serving in the imperial guards of Chang'an in the post-rebellion period than before.[120] In fact, the number of expatriate Sogdian merchants in Chang'an probably increased as well, at least until 780. This was a side effect of the special relationship between the Tang and Uighur empires established during the An Lushan Rebellion. A kind of semi-permanent embassy of some 1,000 Uighur elites and soldiers resided in Chang'an after 757, representing their khaganate's interests and overseeing a trading agreement in which the Tang essentially subsidized the Uighur empire by regularly buying large numbers of horses from it at marked-up prices in silk, silver, and gold. These Uighurs came to view the Tang court's military weakness and dependence on their goodwill with contempt, and frequently committed acts of kidnapping, assault, and looting in the capital during the 770s. Meanwhile, the Sogdian merchants in Central Asia, facing pressures from the Abbasids on one side and the Tibetans on the other, recognized economic opportunity in the Uighurs' newfound power and wealth. Thousands migrated to the walled Uighur capital of Ordu-Balik and began handling its trade in silk with Central Asia. Another 2,000 or so settled in Chang'an, under the protection of the Uighur community, and grew rich by flouting the court's restrictive laws on private commerce with impunity. They were known to disguise themselves in Uighur-style clothing in order to receive the daily food rations to which members of the Uighur diplomatic community were entitled.[121]

---

[119] Zhang, "Tangdai Lingzhou Kangshi."

[120] Bi, *Zhonggu Zhongguo de Sute Huren*, 148–61, 166–67.

[121] *ZZTJ* 224.7218–19, 7221, 225.7228, 7232, 7265, 216.7287–88; *XTS* 217a.6120–21; Vaissière, *Sogdian Traders*, 223–24, 306–309. On the Uighur–Tang trade in horses and silk, see most recently Di Cosmo, "Maligned Exchanges." Di Cosmo argues that the Uighurs did not deliberately sell the Tang inferior horses as the Chinese sources claimed; instead, prolonged drought on the steppe was the reason why many horses arrived in an emaciated state.

Some historians have claimed that the Sogdian expatriates, or their Uighur patrons, engaged in the business of usury.[122] But there is no strong evidence to support this.[123] The only mention of foreign moneylenders in Chang'an occurs in an account of a different diplomatic community: Central Asian ambassadors and their retinues who had been left stranded after their route home was cut off by the Tibetan conquest of Gansu. These Central Asians, like the Uighur community, received free lodging and regular rations, stipends, and subsidies from the Tang court due to their status as foreign dignitaries. Over the years, members of the Central Asian community used their stipends to "lend money on security and profit from the interest" or to buy property such as farmland and houses. They also married local women and began raising children.[124] Tang law ordinarily prohibited imperial subjects from marrying subjects of foreign states (*huawairen*); it is important to emphasize that this law was aimed at avoiding divided loyalties and had nothing to do with ethnic or racial segregation, as it permitted intermarriage between imperial subjects of different ethnicities.[125] But the Central Asians' unusual situation led the imperial court to accord them the privilege of marrying local women and raising their children "like registered [Tang] subjects" – hardly symptomatic of xenophobia! In fact, the court's policy was probably based on a Tang law, introduced in 628, that allowed foreign ambassadors who had been granted an extended stay in Chang'an to marry Tang-subject ("Han") women, provided they leave their local wives behind when finally returning home.[126]

The Sogdian expatriate merchants who resided in Chang'an under Uighur patronage were in a different situation. It was illegal for them to marry Chinese women – or even Sogdian women who were Tang subjects, for that matter – as long as they were neither formally subjects of the Tang empire nor foreign envoys officially permitted to remain in Chang'an for an extended duration. Nor, apparently, could they do so by pretending to be Uighurs, since even Uighur ambassadors and their attendants were apparently not given the legal

---

[122] For example, Xiang, *Tangdai Chang'an yu xiyu wenming*, 46–48, which seems to have been the basis for the notion of "Uighur usurers" (embellished with seemingly imaginary details) in Schafer, *The Golden Peaches of Samarkand*, 20.

[123] On this question see Yang, "Unauthorized Exchanges." [124] *ZZTJ* 232.7492–93.

[125] *TLSY* 8.178. Numerous modern studies have misinterpreted these laws as new restrictions introduced in 836, and therefore claimed them as evidence of late Tang xenophobia. In fact, the document cited in this regard (*CFYG* 99.11562–63) merely says, "according to the statutes and ordinances [*lingshi*], people of the Central Lands are not to have illicit and unauthorized communications, commercial transactions, marriage relations, or interactions with foreigners [*huawai ren*]." It therefore cites preexisting laws rather than introducing new ones. The Tang Code makes it clear that such laws already existed in the seventh century: for example, *TLSY* 8.178.

[126] *TLSY* 8.178; *THY* 100.1796.

privilege of marrying Tang subjects. Consequently, they began taking wives and concubines by pretending to be native-born Tang-subject Sogdians, an identity signaled by dressing in Tang style rather than Uighur style. This was probably not a case of impersonating a different *ethnic group*, as the Sogdians' distinctive Central Asian appearance would have made it difficult for them to pass as Chinese. In 779, the newly enthroned Dezong issued an edict to put an end to such subterfuge by mandating that Uighurs and other foreign (*Fan*) residents in the capital dress in the attire customary to their countries, rather than adopting Chinese-style dress.[127] This may have been a prelude to Dezong's decision to evict the entire Uighur diplomatic community from Chang'an in 780. Many Sogdian merchants probably stayed behind in Chang'an after their Uighur patrons departed, and the court would not have wanted to let them simply blend into the city's Tang-subject Sogdian community by changing clothes.

Dezong's move against the Uighur community of Chang'an was driven by resentment over a traumatic experience that he had suffered in 762, as a young prince tasked with coordinating the second Tang–Uighur assault on Luoyang. Four of his staff officials had refused to let him demean himself by kowtowing to the Uighur khagan Bögü (r. 759–80) and had been flogged on the angry khagan's orders; two had died of their injuries the next day.[128] After their eviction from Chang'an, the Uighurs headed for the steppe with a large baggage train but were massacred near Hohhot, Inner Mongolia, by troops of the Zhenwu Command. Zhenwu military commissioner Zhang Guangsheng (d. 784) had accused them of beating one of his officers and plotting to seize control of Zhenwu, but he was, in reality, driven by resentment of their high-handed behavior and wealth, and hopes of ingratiating himself with the anti-Uighur Dezong. The Sogdians in the Uighur convoy also played a role in instigating Zhang's massacre. A round of political turmoil had recently broken out in the Uighur khaganate: Sogdian merchants in Ordu-Balik had convinced Bögü Khagan to launch a big pillaging raid on the Tang while the Tang court was distracted by Daizong's funeral and Dezong's accession, but the chief minister Tun Bagha Tarkhan (Dun Mohe Dagan), who found this idea foolhardy, assassinated Bögü and took his place as khagan. Several thousand Sogdians were also massacred in the coup, presumably out of anger over their leading the khagan astray. After the Sogdians in the Uighur convoy learned of this massacre, many absconded out of fear of what persecution might await in Ordu-Balik. But after the convoy's commander began preventing Sogdians from leaving, those remaining secretly urged Zhang Guangsheng to kill the Uighurs. Zhang gladly followed their suggestion but ended up massacring

---

[127] *ZZTJ* 225.7265; *THY* 100.1798.   [128] *ZZTJ* 222.7133, 233.7502–04.

them as well, probably because he coveted their wealth. He left just one or two Sogdians alive to return to Ordu-Balik and report the convoy's fate.[129]

The massacre of both Uighurs and Sogdians at Zhenwu cannot be taken as evidence of anti-Sogdian sentiment, though some historians have read it as such.[130] It reflects only Zhang Guangsheng's opportunism and greed and Dezong's anti-Uighur bias. In fact, although Dezong appeased the Uighurs (who demanded compensation for the loss of life and property) by demoting Zhang and paying arrears owed to them in the horse-silk trade, he was also strongly interested in allying with the Tibetans to wage war on them.[131] Only in 787, after his pursuit of a peace covenant with the Tibetan empire had failed spectacularly,[132] did he adopt his chief minister Li Bi's (722–89) proposal for a grand alliance with the Uighurs, Arabs, Indians, and Nanzhao to contain and weaken the Tibetans from every side. The Uighur alliance was quickly renewed via the marriage of one of Dezong's daughters to Tun Bagha Tarkhan. The Uighur khagan was so eager to resume the lucrative horse-silk trade that he agreed to address Dezong as his lord and father, not his brother.[133] Thereafter, the Uighurs began warring with the Tibetans over Central Asia while outwardly accepting Tang suzerainty. When Tang emperor Muzong (r. 820–4) married his younger sister Princess Taihe to the Uighur khagan in 821, the Tibetans were apparently so alarmed by this second renewal of the alliance that they sued for peace.[134] The peace covenant of 821–2 finally ended the long Tang–Tibetan conflict, with both sides recognizing existing borders, ceasing all raids, and agreeing to interact on equal terms on the basis of fictive kinship. A similar Tibetan peace treaty with the Uighurs followed a year later.[135]

Li Bi's grand alliance strategy was quite inspired and appears to have been successful, at least on the Tibetan empire's northern and eastern flanks. In 787, the governor of Jiannan (Sichuan) province began making diplomatic overtures

---

[129] *JTS* 127.3573–74; *XTS* 217a.6121–23; *ZZTJ* 225.7265, 226.7282, 7287–88.

[130] For example, Rong, *Zhonggu Zhongguo yu Sute wenming*, 81–82.

[131] Dezong shielded Zhang Guangsheng from Uighur demands for his execution but demoted him to a non-military post as an act of appeasement. Guangsheng resented this and joined the rebellion of 783–4, for which Dezong did have him put to death.

[132] The Tibetans laid an ambush at a covenant-swearing ceremony in July 787, aiming to kill or capture Qun Jian, who headed the Tang delegation and whom they feared as one of the most effective Tang generals. Qun narrowly escaped, but most of his delegation did not. This disaster strengthened the hand of anti-Tibetan voices at the Tang court.

[133] *ZZTJ* 232.7482–83, 7495, 233.7501–06.

[134] *ZZTJ* 241.7791–92, 242.7799–7800. The war might have ended a decade earlier if Muzong's father Xianzong (r. 805–20) had not consistently rebuffed Uighur requests for a new princess due to the high cost of the dowry (estimated at five million strings of coins): *ZZTJ* 239.7704, 240.7730.

[135] For English translations of the peace covenant texts in Chinese and Tibetan, see Schaeffer *et al.*, eds., *Sources of Tibetan Tradition*, 22–23, 77–78.

to Nanzhao, which soon produced results as its king had grown weary of the Tibetans' frequent demands for tribute and troops. After several years of secret diplomacy, Nanzhao finally returned to the Tang orbit in 794 and began joining in Tang attacks on Tibetan positions.[136] The Tibetans eventually concluded a peace treaty with Nanzhao in 822–3 as well.[137] No military alliance between the Tang and an Indian state seems to have materialized. But Tang sources claim that after 786, the Abbasids began warring with the Tibetans in Central Asia, and that the Tibetans had to divert about half their troops to this new front, reducing the severity of their raids on the Tang and perhaps also slowing down their conquest of the Tarim Basin.[138] Unfortunately, Arabic sources say nothing about any alliance with the Chinese. The recent rediscovery of the epitaph of a Tang eunuch named Yang Liangyao (736–806), which states that he traveled by sea to the Abbasid caliphate in 785 as a Tang ambassador, has led some historians to suggest that Dezong was exploring an anti-Tibetan alliance with the Arabs by then.[139] But given Dezong's pro-Tibetan and anti-Uighur stance until 787, it is also possible that Yang Liangyao's mission was to persuade the Arabs to make war on the Uighur khaganate.

In 787, Li Bi also persuaded Dezong to stop providing stipends and rations to all members of the Central Asian envoy community in Chang'an who owned property, of whom there were now some 4,000. When the Central Asians protested, Li gave them an ultimatum: return to their home countries by sea or via Uighur territory (presumably without their local wives), or stay and earn their keep as salaried members of the Tang military. They all chose the second option and were drafted into the Chang'an-based Shence Army as junior officers or common soldiers (depending on their social status), leaving fewer than twenty Central Asians still eligible for state support. This move reportedly saved the cash-strapped government half a million strings of coins annually.[140] But it had an unintended effect: The Shence Army's enlarged size made it the core of the imperial guards and turned it into a Tang version of the Praetorian Guard during the ninth century. Consistently commanded by powerful eunuchs, it was used against officials and even emperors who threatened eunuch influence at the imperial court. Since, as mentioned earlier, there was also increased recruitment of Sogdians into the imperial guards in the late Tang, this means that the most politically consequential unit in the late Tang military contained large numbers of men of Central Asian descent, including Sogdians.

---

[136] Backus, *The Nan-chao Kingdom*, 87–100.
[137] On the Tibetans' treaties in 822–3 see Iwao, "Kodai Chibetto teikoku no gaikō."
[138] *THY* 100.1790; *JTS* 198.5316; *XTS* 221b.6263.
[139] Schottenhammer, "Yang Liangyao's Mission of 785."   [140] *ZZTJ* 232.7493.

In fact, a bilingual Chinese–Pahlavi epitaph found in Xi'an in 1955 shows that Zoroastrian Iranians, probably descended from Sassanian refugees, also served in the Shence Army and preserved their culture and language as late as 874. The epitaph's subject, a young woman named Māwash (849–74), was from the Iranian Sūrēn (Ch. Suliang) clan, as was her husband, a Shence Army officer. The short Chinese text identifies her as Ms. Ma, wife of Suliang, and states the dates of her birth and death using the Chinese counting system. The Pahlavi text, according to a recent reading, dates her death using three numbering systems: the number of years since the last Sassanian Shahanshah Yazdegerd's accession (242), the year in the Islamic Hijri era (260 AH), and the year in the Xiantong reign era (15) of Tang emperor Yizong (Li Cui, r. 859–73), whom the author hails as "the ever-conquering lord, the Son of God." The author thus demonstrates loyalty to both the Tang and the memory of the Sassanian dynasty, as well as knowledge of Islamic practice. The text ends by professing faith in the primary Zoroastrian deities: Māwash is now "with Ahura Mazda and the Amahraspand in the paradise of light and the superior life."[141] This trace of a bicultural Iranian family living in Chang'an and serving the Tang court on the eve of the Huang Chao Rebellion of 874–84 (on which see the Conclusion) is another piece of evidence against the notion that Tang society took a decidedly xenophobic turn after the An Lushan Rebellion.

5 The Uighur Crisis and the Huichang Persecution of 842–846

Many conventional narratives of Chinese history hold that the Tang empire was in terminal decline after An Lushan's rebellion, fatally weakened by territorial losses and political decentralization. According to this perspective, the Huang Chao Rebellion, which sounded the Tang's death knell, was an inevitable outcome of more than a century of political malaise. But a more careful analysis of Tang political history suggests that the dynasty enjoyed a surprisingly good forty-year stretch from 820 to 860. By 820, the central government had restored direct rule over every province, thanks to the energetic Emperor Xianzong's (r. 805–20) numerous military campaigns against governors who refused to surrender their autonomy.[142] A series of political missteps in 821–2, shortly after Xianzong's death, did result in the outbreak of mutinies in the three major provinces of Hebei, which regained their autonomy and held it until the end of the dynasty. It is interesting to note that in 822, the Uighurs offered to help the Tang attack the Hebei mutineers, but the Tang court declined and paid the khagan off with 70,000 bolts of silk instead, probably due to suspicions that

---

[141] Baghbibi, "New Light on the Middle Persian-Chinese Bilingual Inscription."
[142] Tackett, *The Destruction of the Medieval Chinese Aristocracy*, 146–86.

he was seeking a pretext to pillage Hebei.[143] In 825, Zhaoyi province in southeastern Shanxi also became effectively autonomous and remained so until 844. Nonetheless, the strategic benefits of peace with the Tibetans after 822 more than offset the lack of direct control over four provinces.

It is true that in the 830s, the Tang court was riven by a violent confrontation between powerful eunuchs and their political opponents: the "Sweet Dew Incident" of 835, in which the eunuchs discovered a conspiracy (backed by the emperor himself) to massacre them and, in retaliation, used the Shence Army to slaughter every official connected to it.[144] But this conflict was certainly less destructive than the internal discord that tore both the Tibetan and Uighur empires apart in 839–43. In Tibet, a *tsenpo* was assassinated, generals and nobles split into warring camps, and the plateau descended into centuries of political fragmentation, during which schools of Esoteric Buddhism permanently replaced a unified monarchy as the core of Tibetan cultural identity.[145] The Uighur civil war, according to Tang records, coincided with epidemics and a snowstorm (white *zud*) that killed large numbers of livestock. It ended in 840 with an invasion by the Yenisei Kirghiz people and the Uighur population's dispersal in two general directions: west into Central Asia and the Gansu Corridor; and south to the Tang frontier in Inner Mongolia, northern Shanxi, and northern Hebei.[146]

Uighur refugees in Central Asia eventually founded new states in Turfan, the Tarim Basin, and Gansu, or joined with the Karluks and other western Turkic peoples to build the Karakhanid state (ca. 840–1212). The refugee groups who sought asylum in the Tang were less fortunate. Despite the longstanding Tang–Uighur alliance, on which the Tang had expended three princesses and immense quantities of silk, many Tang officials had long resented the Uighurs' overbearing ways and greeted their downfall with a sense of schadenfreude. The arrival of tens of thousands of Uighur refugees also led some ministers to fear a repeat of the Southern Xiongnu and Eastern Türk revolts of centuries past. Moreover, it emerged that one of the refugee groups, led by *Ögä (Wujie) Khagan (d. 846), was holding Princess Taihe as a hostage. In February 843, Tang troops from the Hedong and Zhenwu commands were ordered to conduct a sneak attack on Ögä's group, which had encamped near Zhenwu. The assault killed about 10,000 Uighurs, took up to 20,000 prisoners, and successfully rescued Princess Taihe. Another 30,000 Uighurs escaped to the Shirwi and Qay with Ögä Khagan, but later deserted him and surrendered peacefully to the Tang governor of autonomous Youzhou. The captured refugees were broken up into

---

[143] *ZZTJ* 242.7814–15.   [144] *ZZTJ* 245.7898–99, 7903–16.
[145] Beckwith, *The Tibetan Empire*, 168–72.
[146] *ZZTJ* 246.7942, 7946–47; *THY* 98.1749; *XTS* 217b.6130–31.

small groups and sent to various provinces to serve as cavalrymen, presumably with the aim of integrating and assimilating them.[147]

In location, execution, and outcome, the attack on the Uighur refugees was quite similar to Li Jing's surprise attack on *Illig Khagan over two centuries earlier, although it was carried out at the imperial court's direction rather than improvised on the spot.[148] Lest one assume that the attack was motivated by simple xenophobia, it should be noted that the Tang cavalry who attacked the Uighurs included thousands of *Kibir (Qibi), Tuygun, Tanguts, and Shatuo Türks, reflecting different paths of migration that had brought these Inner Asian peoples to the northern Shanxi and Ordos frontiers. The Kibir, a Tegreg people, had a long history of fighting for the Tang empire, but also a history of moving between the Tang frontier and the Mongolian steppe. They had migrated to Gansu in 635, moved to Mongolia in 642, re-migrated to Gansu to evade the Eastern Türks around 694, and returned to Mongolia to serve the Uighurs after the Tibetans began conquering Gansu in 765. In 832, "473 tents [i.e., families]" of the Kibir submitted to the Tang and were allowed to settle in Zhenwu, where their leaders – descendants of the renowned early Tang general Kibir *Garik (Qibi Heli) – eventually rose to the position of military commissioner.[149] The Tuygun and Tanguts who participated in the attack on the Uighurs were descended from groups that had migrated into Tang territory in the late seventh and eighth centuries to escape conquest by the Tibetans. They had eventually been moved into the Ordos and northern Shanxi regions to keep them safe from Tibetan raids, and perhaps also to remove the temptation to defect. The Shatuo, originally inhabitants of the Dzungarian Basin, had been resettled in Gansu by the Tibetan empire in the 790s, then migrated to the Ordos around 808 and submitted to the Tang. Resettled in northern Shanxi in 809, they had merged with the Turco-Sogdian community there (which, as previously noted, had itself been resettled from the Ordos in 786) and grown into the Tang army's most formidable cavalry unit.[150] Some of these Inner Asian frontier populations had a somewhat complicated relationship with the Tang government; the Tanguts, in particular, were prone to rebelling when abused by corrupt officials. But they all viewed the influx of Uighur

---

[147] For a detailed study of the refugee crisis, see Drompp, *Tang China and the Collapse of the Uighur Empire*.

[148] See Yang, *Early Tang China and the World*, Section 2.

[149] *ZZTJ* 246.7967; Dong, "An-Shi zhi luan hou Hexi Tiele buzu de qianxi."

[150] The Shatuo helped a renegade minister to overthrow the Uighur khagan at the beginning of the Uighur civil war, in exchange for a gift of 300 horses: *ZZTJ* 246.7942. On the origins and early history of the Shatuo, see Moribe, "Tōmatsu Godai no Daihoku"; Barenghi, "Representations of Descent"; Barenghi, "The Making of the Shatuo."

immigrants as a threat to their interests and proactively volunteered their services in helping the Tang to eliminate it.[151]

Soon after the attack on Ögä Khagan's Uighurs, Emperor Wuzong (Li Yan, r. 840–6) expressed interest in having the Kirghiz seize the Tarim and Dzungarian basins from the Uighurs and return them to the Tang. His ministers dissuaded him on the grounds that since those regions were still cut off from the empire, it would be logistically impracticable to deploy garrisons to them. In 844, the court shifted to formulating plans for the reconquest of Gansu and eastern Qinghai, taking advantage of the Tibetan empire's collapse; this would presumably open the possibility of rebuilding the lost empire in Central Asia.[152] In 843–4, Wuzong also launched a military campaign to subdue autonomous Zhaoyi province; this eventually succeeded, but at a steep cost that the Japanese monk-pilgrim Ennin (793–864), perhaps with some exaggeration, put at 200,000 strings of coins per day.[153] It was in this context that Wuzong began his infamous persecution of Buddhism and three other religions of Iranian origin (Manichaeism, East Syriac or "Nestorian" Christianity, and Zoroastrianism) that, unlike Buddhism, were generally practiced only by communities of Iranian or Sogdian immigrants and expatriates in the Tang.[154] This "Huichang persecution," named after Wuzong's only reign era, ended upon his death in 846.

Historians have debated the causes of the Huichang persecution since the 1950s. In a classic study of the detailed diary that Ennin kept in China in 838–47 (a valuable firsthand account of Wuzong's reign from a Buddhist foreigner's perspective), Edwin Reischauer proposed that the main cause was economic rather than religious: The tax-exempt Buddhist monastic community (*sangha*) had become extremely rich in land, manpower, and other forms of wealth, due to centuries of generous donations from the state and elite families and the attractive (for some) option of evading taxation by becoming a monk. Closing monasteries, confiscating their property (including serfs and slaves), melting their bronze images and bells down to make coins, and laicizing monks and nuns was, according to this logic, primarily a means for the perennially cash-strapped late Tang state to restore its fiscal health and secure new resources for

---

[151] *ZZTJ* 246.7952.   [152] *ZZTJ* 247.7974, 7999–8000.

[153] Reischauer, trans., *Ennin's Diary*, 337, 346.

[154] East Syriac Christianity, also known as the Church of the East, was the official church of Sassanian Iran from 410, but was rejected as heretical by the churches of the Roman empire after the Nestorian controversy of 431. It was introduced to the Tang by an Iranian missionary in 635, according to the famous bilingual "Nestorian Stele" inscription erected in Chang'an in 781 (and rediscovered by Jesuit missionaries in 1623). Modern study of Christianity's history in the Tang is a distinct subfield centered on analysis of this inscription and several religious texts found in the Dunhuang library cave. A Christian inscription in Chinese from Luoyang, dated 815, was also discovered in 2006. See Nicolini-Zani, *The Luminous Way to the East*.

military campaigns and other costly projects.[155] This interpretation gained the support of Kenneth Ch'en and other scholars, who noted that Wuzong's predecessors had already recognized the Buddhist establishment's drain on the state's resources and tried to address the problem by limiting the ordination of new monks and nuns, banning the founding of new monasteries, and laicizing clergy who failed a basic test in sutra recitation.[156] Indeed, Ennin's diary indicates that Wuzong's early measures against Buddhism in 842–3 were limited to such conventional regulations.[157] An edict that Wuzong issued in 845, announcing the laicization of nearly all the empire's Buddhist monks and nuns and the confiscation of their property, also placed much emphasis on the economic benefits to the people.[158]

But economic considerations clearly cannot account for all aspects of the persecution. After all, Wuzong did not take similar measures against the Daoist clergy, who had considerable wealth as well; instead, he extended lavish patronage to Daoism while persecuting Buddhism. Moreover, the Christian and Zoroastrian clergy numbered only 3,000 or so and were hardly equal to the Buddhist and Daoist establishments in wealth. Why would Wuzong also target them for laicization in 845, claiming that they were "adulterating the customs of the Hua (Chinese) of the Central Lands?"[159] Given that the size of the Manichaean community was similarly small, why did Wuzong issue orders to laicize all Manichaean priests in Chang'an and Luoyang, burn their scriptures and images, and confiscate their property in March 843?[160] And why, according to Ennin's diary, did he issue an edict ordering the execution of these same priests two months later – unusually harsh treatment not meted out to Zoroastrians, Christians, or even Buddhists?[161]

That brings us to the other secondary factors that Reischauer identified for the persecution. One of these was the literati ruling elite's supposed secular and "rationalistic" bias, derived from Confucian humanist thought, against Buddhism as an anti-familial, immoral, and superstitious faith. The other was a version of the then-popular notion of a late Tang xenophobic turn: "a rising nationalistic reaction against anything foreign," triggered by "barbarian incursions" during the "long period of T'ang decline."[162] Both factors are still often cited in general narratives of Chinese history, but have long been disproven by scholarship demonstrating the intensity and pervasiveness of both Buddhist and

---

[155] Reischauer, *Ennin's Travels*, 218.
[156] Ch'en, "The Economic Background of the Hui-ch'ang Suppression"; Weinstein, *Buddhism under the T'ang*, 107–14.
[157] Reischauer, *Ennin's Diary*, 321–25.
[158] *JTS* 18a.605–606. A full translation can be found in Reischauer, *Ennin's Travels*, 225–27.
[159] Ibid.   [160] *JTS* 18a.594; *XTS* 217b.6133.   [161] Reischauer, *Ennin's Diary*, 327.
[162] Reischauer, *Ennin's Travels*, 219–20.

Daoist devotion among Tang literati throughout the late eighth and ninth centuries, despite the disapproval of a small minority of Confucian purists like Han Yu (768–824). The Tang elite was hardly as secular or rationalistic as Reischauer assumed it to be.

In fact, far from blaming the "foreign" religion of Buddhism for the An Lushan Rebellion or deriding it as irrational or superstitious, the Tang court became more pro-Buddhist after the An Lushan Rebellion than before. Emperor Daizong's pro-Buddhist chief ministers convinced him that good karma from the Tang dynasty's past patronage of the *sangha* had allowed it to outlast the rebellions of An Lushan and Buqut Huai'en, and that continued patronage would similarly protect it from Tibetan invasions. Daizong thereupon greatly increased the court's donations to Buddhist monasteries, and extended immunity from corporal punishment (previously a privilege for officials and their families only) to monks and nuns throughout the empire. Whenever Tibetan raids were reported, he had monks recite the Indian Esoteric Buddhist master Amoghavajra's (705–74) new version of the *Prajnaparamita Scripture for Humane Kings Who Wish to Protect Their States*, rewarding the monks richly once the raiders departed.[163] Amoghavajra was already credited with saving the Tang by performing tantric rites that supposedly caused Buqut Huai'en's sudden demise in 765. The Indian monk's status as a kind of imperial preceptor at Daizong's court perhaps represented the zenith of Buddhism's use as a protective and legitimating force in Tang politics, leading Charles Orzech to call him "the most powerful monk in Chinese history."[164] As Stanley Weinstein noted, "Although the idea that Buddhism could afford protection to the state was advocated in one form or another by most leading monks since the fifth century, it reached its pinnacle during the reign of [Daizong]."[165]

The Tang court continued to see patronizing Buddhism as vital to the empire's security long after the deaths of Amoghavajra and Daizong. From 760 to 819, the court maintained a tradition of having a Buddha fingerbone relic, normally housed in the Famen Temple, brought into Chang'an to be displayed and venerated every thirty years. Although Gaozong and Empress Wu had also venerated the Famen relic, this practice took on much greater importance in late Tang times, as it was now believed to bring the empire a new karmic

---

[163] *ZZTJ* 224.7196; *JTS* 118.3417–18; Weinstein, *Buddhism under the T'ang*, 77–89. Amoghavajra, also known by the Chinese translation of his monastic name, Bukong Jinggang, was one of the teachers of Hyecho (on whom see Yang, *Early Tang China and the World*, Section 7). On his career and the *Scripture for Humane Kings*, see also Orzech, *Politics and Transcendent Wisdom*; Goble, *Chinese Esoteric Buddhism*.

[164] Orzech, "Esoteric Buddhism in the Tang," 281.

[165] Weinstein, *Buddhism under the T'ang*, 82.

dispensation of peace and prosperity.[166] Han Yu's famous 819 memorial to Xianzong, in which he denigrated the Buddha as a barbarian and called for the bone to be destroyed, is often taken as reflecting the xenophobic spirit of his age.[167] But we know from other sources that Han Yu directed polemics against both Buddhism and Daoism, rejecting them as immoral and inimical to Chinese civilization and calling for them to be proscribed, and that his views were regarded as outrageously extreme and narrow-minded by most of his peers.[168] Han Yu's Confucian exclusivist views became more popular in the eleventh century under the Song dynasty, due to a revival of interest in imitating both his powerful prose style and his critique of ideological pluralism.[169] But rigid Confucian exclusivism was never state policy in either Tang or Song, and it is simply wrong to project Han Yu's personal prejudices onto late Tang society at large. Consider that in 871, when the Famen relic was rediscovered in a hidden tunnel where it had been concealed to prevent it from being destroyed during the Huichang persecution, Emperor Yizong enthusiastically ordered that veneration of the relic be revived on the same grand scale as before.[170]

If Wuzong was not riding a groundswell of xenophobic sentiment, what explains his consistent public use of Buddhism's "barbarian" origins as a justification for persecuting it and insisting that his ministers and subjects stop practicing it? Here we come to Reischauer's argument that Wuzong was a "Taoist [Daoist] fanatic" and that this was the source of the "special ferocity" of his anti-Buddhist campaign.[171] Both Ennin's diary and Tang sources make it quite evident that Wuzong was under the influence of Daoist priest-alchemists who had promised him an elixir that would enable him to become a *xian* (immortal/transcendent): the state of deathless, weightless semi-divinity that Daoists saw as the ultimate plane of existence.[172] Although Wuzong was only thirty in 844 and seemingly had no reason to become obsessed with living forever, he was hardly alone among ninth-century Tang emperors in this regard. His grandfather Xianzong and his father Muzong (Li Heng, r. 820–4) had both died at a relatively young age of health complications resulting from elixir consumption, and so would Wuzong himself and his successor Xuānzong (Li Chen, r. 846–59). Yizong's sudden death at the age of forty, just three-and-a-half

---

[166] Sen, "Relic Worship at the Famen Temple"; Sen, *Buddhism, Diplomacy, and Trade*, 64–74.

[167] Xianzong was enraged by Han Yu's blasphemy, as well as his inauspicious insinuation that venerating the relic would shorten Xianzong's life, and had him banished to the far south. For the text of the memorial, see Ma, *Han Changli wenji jiaozhu*, 683–88. For a full translation, see Mair *et al.*, eds., *Hawaii Reader in Traditional Chinese Culture*, 355–57.

[168] Yang, *The Way of the Barbarians*, 5–7, 24–56.   [169] Ibid., 74–97.

[170] Sen, *Buddhism, Diplomacy, and Trade*, 74; Chen, "A Chinese Monk under a 'Barbarian' Mask?" 114–23.

[171] Reischauer, *Ennin's Travels*, 220.

[172] Ibid., 243–53; *ZZTJ* 248.8020–21. See also Weinstein, *Buddhism under the T'ang*, 115–16.

months after venerating the Famen relic in 873, is left unexplained in the sources, but it is likely to have had something to do with elixirs as well. Given this track record of cutting emperors down in their prime, one would expect Daoism, not Buddhism, to be hated and persecuted instead. Yet our sources tell us that the Daoist alchemists used Wuzong's desire for immortality to convince him to transfer to Daoist institutions the state patronage previously accorded to Buddhism. Wuzong even commanded Imperial College students and civil service examination candidates to begin studying the Daoist canon alongside the Confucian classics.[173]

Wuzong's anti-Buddhist policies were thus rooted in long-running competition between the Buddhist and Daoist clerical establishments for imperial patronage, one in which Daoists frequently employed ethnocentric arguments to assert that a Chinese religion had to be superior to one from the barbarians, or at least better suited to the Chinese.[174] Ennin also tells us that the Daoists actively poisoned Wuzong's mind against Buddhism: They cited a prophecy that implied that monks would seize the throne from him, and they claimed in 845 that the *qi* imbalance caused by Buddhism's continued existence in China was blocking Wuzong's path to immortality, even when he ascended the massive "transcendent terrace" that he had constructed on their advice. Ennin claims that Wuzong then resolved to eradicate Buddhism from his empire completely.[175] It is possible that his actions against Christianity and Zoroastrianism flowed from the same belief that the cosmologically polluting presence of foreign religions in China was hindering the efficacy of his Daoist elixirs and rites – hence his declaration in 845 that "as for the temples of the Daqin [Romans, i.e., Christians] and Muhu [Magi, i.e., Zoroastrians], now that the teaching of Sakyamuni [i.e., Buddhism] has been eliminated, these heterodox doctrines cannot be allowed to remain."[176]

As for why Wuzong began persecuting Manichaean priests in the two Tang capitals in 843, not long after Ögä Khagan's defeat, it is possible that he suspected them of being a potential fifth column for the fugitive Ögä and other Uighur refugee groups still active beyond the frontier. Manichaeism had been the Uighur khaganate's official religion since the 760s, and the Uighur khagans were known to use Manichaean priests as advisors. Most of the Manichaean priests in the Tang capitals had arrived with Uighur diplomatic

---

[173] *ZZTJ* 247.8000, 8015; Reischauer, *Ennin's Diary*, 340–42, 344, 347–48, 351–53. Wuzong's addition of Daoism to the examination curriculum was not unprecedented: the pro-Daoist Xuanzong had earlier tried establishing a parallel system of schooling and examinations in the Daoist philosophical classics.

[174] Abramson, *Ethnic Identity in Tang China*, 52–82.

[175] Reischauer, *Ennin's Diary*, 342–43, 354–58; Weinstein, *Buddhism under the T'ang*, 123–29.

[176] *JTS* 18a.605.

missions and resided in temples established with Uighur patronage. The Tang court had once expelled them all in 817, apparently because they had colluded with merchants in Chang'an to flout the empire's laws against private trade with the Uighurs.[177] But they had later been allowed to return. According to Ennin, Wuzong now ordered his officials to tonsure the (already forcibly laicized) priests and dress them up as Buddhist monks before killing them, perhaps to cover up their murders and thus avoid alienating Uighurs who had already surrendered to the Tang.[178] Reischauer, while doubting the historicity of this massacre, correctly surmised that "the persecution of Manichaeanism was at least in part because it was the religion of the Turkish Uighurs of Central Asia."[179]

Since the 1990s, numerous studies have debunked the myth (once believed uncritically by Wright, Reischauer, and many others) that the Huichang persecution sent Chinese Buddhism into permanent decline. The Buddhist monastic establishment, though hit hard by mass monastery closures and property confiscations, soon recovered fully thanks to generous support from Wuzong's successors.[180] One can safely assume that most monasteries were reopened and that the vast majority of forcibly laicized monks and nuns quickly returned to monastic life.[181] The persecution's impact on the three other foreign religions was apparently not fatal either, though many modern accounts claim that it was.[182] As we saw earlier, there was clearly still a Zoroastrian community in Chang'an as late as 874; recent research by Chinese scholar Zhang Xiaogui also shows that elements of Zoroastrian worship underwent indigenization and survived as a part of local religion in north China during the Song period.[183] A fugitive Manichaean priest is said to have brought his religion to southeast China during the Huichang persecution, and it acquired a local following that apparently survived until the early seventeenth century – long outliving Manichaeism in Iran and Central Asia, which died out in the tenth and eleventh centuries.[184] East Syriac Christianity had no significant presence in subsequent Chinese dynasties before being reintroduced under the Mongol empire, but this

---

[177] *ZZTJ* 237.7638, 240.7730.

[178] Reischauer, *Ennin's Diary*, 327; *pace* Weinstein, *Buddhism under the T'ang*, 121, which suggested this was meant as "a grim warning to the Chinese Buddhist clergy of things to come."

[179] Reischauer, *Ennin's Travels*, 232.   [180] Weinstein, *Buddhism under the T'ang*, 136–44.

[181] Benjamin Brose has shown that Buddhist institutions in Chang'an and Luoyang recovered quickly from the Huichang persecution but were eventually forced to relocate to south China after Huang Chao's rebels took the capitals in 880–1 and destroyed or looted many monasteries. The transplanted monks then received patronage from regional warlords in the south. Brose, *Patrons and Patriarchs*, 30–47.

[182] For example, Forte, "Iranians in China," 280–81.

[183] Zhang, *Zhongguo huahua xianjiao kaoshu*.

[184] Gulácsi, "A Manichaean 'Portrait of the Buddha Jesus'"; Kósa, "Mānī on the Margins."

may not be due solely to the Huichang persecution.[185] Modern historians have tended to make much of tenth-century Arabic accounts of a massacre of 120,000 or 200,000 "Muslims, Jews, Christians, and Zoroastrians" in Guangzhou by the rebel army of Huang Chao (*Bānshū* in Arabic) in 879, misreading this as another example of "late Tang xenophobia" even though the accounts claim that the rebels also massacred the Chinese population of Guangzhou.[186] The Arabic authors claimed to have based the number of foreign dead on Chinese government records, but more careful historians believe the numbers to be greatly exaggerated.[187] Tang records do not mention a massacre in Guangzhou at all, noting only that some 30–40 percent of the rebel army died of malaria while holding the city.[188] In any case, if there is any truth to the Arabic accounts of the Guangzhou massacre, this would indirectly show that Christian and Zoroastrian communities in the Tang survived the 840s and that some, unfortunately, then perished during the Huang Chao Rebellion.

I would suggest that because Islam was practiced only by Arab and Iranian merchant communities in south China under the Tang, it was virtually unknown to the Tang court and thus excluded from the Huichang persecution. It seems likely that Christianity was the only Abrahamic religion with a presence in Chang'an, due to its existence in the Sogdian community. The Arab writer Abu Zayd al-Sirafi, writing in the early tenth century, tells the story of one Ibn Wahb who sailed from Iran to Guangzhou sometime after 871 and then traveled to Chang'an, where he met the Tang emperor himself. The emperor turned out to have considerable knowledge about the prophets of Islam, and a casket filled with pictures of them. Much of this story is probably literary invention, as extant Tang sources (e.g., Du Huan's account) give no indication of such familiarity with Islam as a religion. Nor is it likely that a Tang emperor would acknowledge Iraq as the center of the world and its king (the Abbasid caliph) as the greatest of the world's rulers, as Ibn Wahb (or Abu Zayd) claimed.[189] Islam only became a major religion in China from the mid-thirteenth century on, after large numbers of Central Asians and Iranians arrived as soldiers and administrators for the Mongol empire and established permanent communities in both north and south. These communities later erected Sinographic inscriptions in their mosques that often traced their histories, as well as the founding of the mosques themselves, to the early Tang period. But most modern scholars doubt the veracity of such claims, especially when they pertain to north Chinese

---

[185] For a discussion of possible reasons for the disappearance of Christianity from post-Tang China, see Nicolini-Zani, *The Luminous Way to the East*, 77–84.
[186] al-Sirafi, *Accounts of China and India*, 30.
[187] Chaffee, *The Muslim Merchants of Premodern China*, 47–49.   [188] *ZZTJ* 253.8217.
[189] al-Sirafi, *Accounts of China and India*, 36–39.

cities.[190] A famous inscription in a mosque in Xi'an (formerly Chang'an), supposedly composed by the Tang minister Wang Hong (d. 752) in 742, is generally also rejected by modern scholars as a Ming-era forgery, though Chinese historians remain reluctant to rule out the existence of a Muslim community in Tang Chang'an due to the idea's importance to the historical memory of the Sinitic Muslim (Hui) population.[191]

Judaism was similarly unfamiliar to the Tang elite. The existence of a Jewish community in late Tang Guangzhou appears to be corroborated by the ninth-century Abbasid geographer Ibn Khurradādhbih (ca. 820–912), who claimed that Jewish maritime merchants sailed from the Red Sea to India and China, returning with musk, camphor, cinnamon, and other such products purchased from the Chinese.[192] There is manuscript evidence of Persian-speaking Jewish merchants in the Khotan area by the late eighth century, and a copy of a Hebrew prayer (perhaps used as a protective talisman) was found in the Dunhuang library cave.[193] But whether Jews lived in any city of the late Tang heartland remains in doubt. The famous community of Jews in Kaifeng is generally believed to have settled there in the Song dynasty, not the Tang; a recent study argues that its actual beginnings should be dated even later, to the Ming (1368–1644).[194]

6 Tang China and the Making of the Sinographic Sphere

In 799, Jiannan provincial governor Wei Gao (745–805) began a program of educating young men from the Nanzhao aristocracy in the schools of the provincial capital, Chengdu, with the provincial government covering all expenses involved (e.g., meals and lodging). Each class of Nanzhao students would graduate upon mastering Sinographic literacy and mathematics, to be replaced by a new cohort.[195] The program of educational diplomacy continued for more than fifty years and was a variation on the Tang court's longstanding policy of allowing elite men from tributary states to enroll in the Imperial

---

[190] Steinhardt, *China's Early Mosques*, 8–9, 34; Chaffee, *The Muslim Merchants of Premodern China*, 19–20.

[191] See, for example, Lin, "Yuanmao suishi, wenwei shizhen."

[192] Silverstein, "From Markets to Marvels." Silverstein argues that Jewish merchants stopped sailing to China for good after the massacre in Guangzhou. Arabic sources suggest that Muslim merchants also avoided Guangzhou and relocated their operations to Southeast Asia for about a century after the massacre: Chaffee, *The Muslim Merchants of Premodern China*, 51–65.

[193] For discussion and translation of the relevant documents, see Hansen, *The Silk Road*, 302, 325, 357–59, 381–82.

[194] Yu, "Revising the Date of Jewish Arrival in Kaifeng."

[195] The sources disagree on whether Wei Gao did this on his own initiative or at the insistence of the king of Nanzhao. *ZZTJ* 249.8078; *XTS* 222a.6276; Backus, *The Nan-chao Kingdom*, 101–102.

College in Chang'an. Wei Gao simply based it in Chengdu due to the large amount of autonomy that the Tang court gave him over the administration of Sichuan and relations with Nanzhao during his twenty-year term as governor (785–805).[196]

Around the year 821, the Tang empire officially opened the most prestigious *jinshi* (presented scholar) category of its civil service examinations to candidates from foreign countries, who would be known as "guest candidates" (*bingong*). Guest candidates had to take the standard *jinshi* examination, consisting of poetry composition, tests on passages from the Confucian classics, and policy essays. But whereas the *jinshi* typically had a very low pass quota of 1–2 percent for Chinese candidates, foreign candidates had their own quota which, due to their small numbers, effectively made their chances of passing much better. Most guest candidates attempted the examinations after years of study at the Imperial College in Chang'an. Men from the Manchurian state of Bohai (including a chief minister of that kingdom) and an Arab immigrant are known to have passed, but Silla men, who made up the majority of foreign students at the Imperial College, naturally produced the largest number of guest candidates.[197] Silla had created its own civil service examination system in 788, modeled after that of the Tang, but the kingdom's bone rank system of aristocratic castes continued to reserve all high ministerial posts for men of the true-bone caste. This may have motivated ambitious men of the next highest caste, known as head rank six, to pursue the more prestigious path of examination success in the Tang, which might result in a higher position in Silla or even a post in the Tang bureaucracy. By the end of the Tang dynasty, at least fifty-eight guest candidates from Silla had passed the *jinshi*, of whom the best known is Choe Chiwon (857–d. after 908). In 869 Choe's father (a man of head rank six status) sent him to the Tang to study in the Imperial College at the age of twelve, reportedly threatening to disown him if he did not pass the *jinshi* within ten years. Choe earned his *jinshi* degree within five years and spent the next decade as a minor official of the collapsing Tang empire before returning to serve his home country. Back in Silla, his lack of true-bone status still prevented him from realizing his political ambitions. Choe finally retired to a life of reclusion while Silla itself collapsed in a period of rebellion and civil war (889–936), out of which would emerge the slightly more meritocratic state of Goryeo (Koryŏ).[198]

---

[196] It was Wei whose diplomatic efforts had won Nanzhao back from the Tibetan fold in 787–94.

[197] Dang, *Tang yu Xinluo*, 49–60; Yang, *The Way of the Barbarians*, 59–62. As of 837, there were 216 students from Silla in Chang'an: *THY* 36.668. On Bohai and its relations with the Tang, see Yang, *Early Tang China and the World*, Section 5.

[198] Oh, "Two Shilla Intellectuals in Tang."

It is widely believed that the Japanese Abe no Nakamaro (698–770) passed the *jinshi* in 727, long before the guest candidate category existed. However, Murakami Tetsumi points out that there is no reliable evidence that Nakamaro ever took the Tang examinations.[199] Nonetheless, the clearly gifted Nakamaro, who went by the name Chao Heng in China, did spend ten years studying in the Imperial College. He was then appointed to posts in the civil bureaucracy rather than the military – a distinction shared by few other foreigners at the time – and befriended numerous prominent men of letters in Chang'an, including poets Wang Wei (ca. 699–761) and Li Bai (or Li Bo, 701–62).[200] In 733, he requested permission to return to Japan, only to be turned down by Xuanzong. Kibi no Makibi (695–775), who arrived in China with Nakamaro in 717, did obtain permission to return in 735 and quickly became highly influential at the Japanese court thanks to the knowledge of the Confucian classics, Chinese history, and Tang law that he had acquired in Chang'an.[201] One could argue that Makibi was luckier in being less impressive than Nakamaro. Twenty years later, in 752, Nakamaro finally obtained Xuanzong's approval to depart with a returning tribute mission led by Fujiwara no Kiyokawa (b. 706) and Kibi no Makibi. Unfortunately, he boarded Kiyokawa's ship, which was blown off course to north Vietnam. The mission's three other ships did manage to reach Japan: The Chinese monk Jianzhen was on one of them, while Makibi was on another.[202] Nakamaro and Kiyokawa returned to Chang'an in 755, only to flee from An Lushan's rebels with Xuanzong's court in 756. Abandoning all hope of going home in the ensuing turmoil, Nakamaro served in various posts, including protector-general of Annan (north Vietnam), before dying in retirement in Chang'an. Kiyokawa, too, remained in China permanently and served in the Tang government, even marrying a Chinese woman and having a daughter.[203]

No Japanese man is known to have become a *jinshi* guest candidate in the ninth century. The main reason may have been that by the early ninth century, simply joining a tribute mission to China and returning alive was enough to earn a Japanese official a generous promotion in rank at the Heian court.[204] The added investment of spending many years studying for the examinations in Chang'an may not have seemed worthwhile to an ambitious young aristocrat,

---

[199] Murakami, "Abei Zhongmalü yu Tangdai shiren," 91.   [200] Ibid., 90–96.

[201] Another member of the 717 Japanese student cohort, known to the Chinese as Jing Zhencheng (699–734), died in Chang'an in the year of Makibi's return to Japan; his epitaph was unearthed in 2004. On Makibi and Jing Zhencheng, see Wang, "Jing Zhencheng yu Abei Zhongmalü, Jibei Zhenbei," 60–65.

[202] On Jianzhen, see Yang, *Early Tang China and the World*, Section 7.

[203] His daughter left for Japan with a returning Japanese tribute mission in 778, and barely survived the passage when a storm broke the ship in half. *Shoku nihongi* 続日本紀, Chapter 35.

[204] Wang, *Ambassadors from the Islands of Immortals*, 60–65.

given that social connections in Heian, often secured through marriage, were more important to his prospects of advancement. In addition, the prestige of examination success waned in Japan over the course of the ninth century, as the five highest court ranks were monopolized by a small core of aristocratic families (not unlike Silla's bone rank system). For appointments to high office, noble birth came to take precedence over non-hereditary measures of merit such as classical learning and administrative ability, causing Japan's own versions of the examination system and Imperial College to decline into irrelevance.[205] Having no need to prove their qualifications for government service, most Japanese aristocrats took no interest in classical learning and focused on displays of literary refinement, often through allusions to or imitations of Tang poetry. Copies of the Chinese literary anthologies relevant to such arts could now be obtained via trade, without braving the dangers of a tribute mission. The most notable instance of this was the work of the prolific poet Bai Juyi (or Bo Juyi, 772–846), which attained instant popularity in Japan upon being introduced and remained popular for at least three centuries.[206]

The Bai Juyi mania in Japan was facilitated by the expansion of East Asian maritime trade during the early ninth century, largely carried by Silla ships and facilitated by the emergence of Silla merchant communities along the Shandong and Huainan coasts.[207] Yuan Zhen's (779–831) preface to the 824 edition of Bai Juyi's collected works, the *Changqing-era Collection of Mr. Bai's Works* (*Baishi Changqing ji*), claims that Bai's poems had already become highly popular in Silla, leading to a poetry-buying spree among Silla merchants. Japan's first encounter with Bai Juyi's poetry came through an anthology of his and Yuan Zhen's poetry that arrived on a merchant ship in 838, probably crewed by Silla Koreans. The Japanese monk Egaku (fl. 835–64) gained access to an expanded edition of Bai Juyi's works held at the Nanchan Temple in Suzhou, Jiangsu in 844 and brought a copy of it back to Japan in 846–7, presumably also on a Silla ship.[208] Japanese tribute missions stopped traveling to China after 839, as the Japanese court lost interest in participating in the Chinese tributary system. Ennin was thus one of the last Japanese monks to travel to China with a tribute mission. But other Japanese monks continued to make the journey on Korean and Chinese merchant vessels: For example, Egaku traveled to China two more times in the 850s. Monks and merchants thus became the main agents of Sino-Japanese interaction and remained so until the thirteenth century.[209]

---

[205] McMullen, *The Worship of Confucius in Japan*, 64–67.
[206] Smits, "Reading the New Ballads."
[207] The significance of these communities was first raised by Reischauer, *Ennin's Travels*, 274–94.
[208] Smits, "Reading the New Ballads," 169–70; Chen, "Hui'e dongchuan 'Baishi wenji.'"
[209] Li, "Shi zhi shisan shiji Zhong-Ri jiaoliu."

These cases of cross-cultural exchange show that over the course of the seventh to ninth centuries, diplomatic, educational, commercial, and religious interactions between the Tang and some of its neighbors resulted in a cultural or civilizational sphere defined by an elite culture of reading and composing texts in the Literary Sinitic language (i.e., Classical Chinese), using the non-phonetic Sinographic script. Elite men from different countries within this sphere could communicate through the written word even though they spoke mutually unintelligible languages; Sinographic writing thus served as a kind of "scripta franca." Countries within the sphere also tended to share political ideologies and institutions derived from the Tang imperial model, including state patronage of Buddhism and reverence for the Confucian classics. Here, I will call this ecumene the Sinographic sphere, but scholars have given it various other names including the East Asian cultural sphere, the *kanji* cultural sphere (*kanji* being the Japanese word for Sinographs), the Sinosphere, and the Sinographic cosmopolis.[210] The last of these terms was inspired by Sheldon Pollock's thesis of the "Sanskrit cosmopolis," a large region encompassing numerous states in South and Southeast Asia that, from roughly 300 to 1300, shared an elite political and literary culture shaped by classic texts written and read in the Sanskrit language (e.g., the *Ramayana*), albeit using different Indic writing systems (Figure 6).[211]

The Chinese empires were never a part of the Sanskrit cosmopolis, as literacy in Sanskrit was rare among the Chinese literati elite and even the Chinese Buddhist monastic community. But several centuries' worth of state-sponsored sutra translation projects made it possible for China to become an alternative core in the Buddhist world, one that served as a medium for Buddhism's spread to other Sinographic states in East Asia, where Sanskrit mostly served only as an incomprehensible magical language used in Buddhist *dharanis* and mantras (i.e., incantations). Whereas Buddhist scriptures were translated into Literary Sinitic in large numbers, the converse was not true: Literary Sinitic texts like the Confucian classics and dynastic histories were not widely translated into non-Sinographic writing systems either before or during the Tang period, excepting an abortive effort by emperor Taizong to spread Daoism to India by having the *Laozi Daodejing* translated into Sanskrit.[212] Acquiring Sinographic literacy was thus essential to accessing and mastering the contents of these texts.

The ruling elites of the Korean kingdoms (Goguryeo, Baekje, Silla) became literate in Literary Sinitic in the two to three centuries preceding the Tang, with Chinese immigrants, Buddhist monks, and officials from the former Chinese

---

[210] King, "Ditching 'Diglossia'"; Denecke and Nguyen, "Shared Literary Heritage in the East Asian Sinographic Sphere."
[211] Pollock, *The Language of the Gods*.   [212] Sen, *Buddhism, Diplomacy, and Trade*, 40.

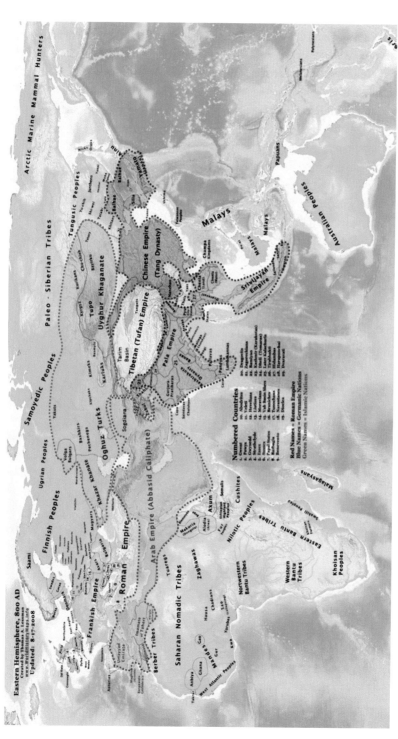

Figure 6 Approximate boundaries of the Sinographic sphere (red), Sanskrit cosmopolis (blue), Turkic world (brown), and Islamic world (green) in 800 CE. Base map from www.worldhistorymaps.info; modified by the author.

colonies in Korea all likely playing a role in this process. The Japanese began acquiring literacy in the fifth century, via influence from Baekje, before seeking Sinitic texts and both classical and Buddhist learning directly from the Sui and Tang. Bohai acquired the foundations of Sinographic literacy from its Goguryeo immigrant population and also sent students to the Imperial College in Chang'an (though in smaller numbers than its rival Silla). Lastly, the Nanzhao royal family first gained literacy from Zheng Hui, a Tang local official captured in 757 and appointed as royal tutor;[213] Wei Gao's educational program then made it available to the kingdom's entire elite in the first half of the ninth century. In each of these cases, the indigenous elites had no system of writing prior to the introduction of the Sinographic system. In the cases of Silla and Japan, Sinographic writing was also adapted to transcribe the indigenous language; in Japan, the *man'yōgana* transcription system evolved into the simpler *hiragana* and *katakana* syllabaries during the eighth and ninth centuries. A late eighth-century funerary inscription found in Lijiang, Yunnan suggests that the Brahmic Tibetan script was introduced to Nanzhao during its period of Tibetan vassalage (750–94), but, if so, its elite subsequently renounced that influence so fully that it has left no other trace.[214]

It's worth pondering why the Sinographic sphere only expanded into East Asia and Yunnan during the Tang period, despite the military and political influence that the Tang projected into Inner Asia before 755. The main reason seems to be that in Asian states where alphabetic/abjadic or abugidic writing systems (e.g., Sogdian, Arabic, Brahmic, Kharosthi) were already in use or were introduced at around the same time as Sinographic writing, Sinographic literacy generally did not take hold – most likely because it took much more effort to achieve. Those parts of Asia thus remained outside the Sinographic sphere and largely untouched by the influence of Chinese civilization. Indic writing systems were the norm in Tibet and Southeast Asia, except for Chinese-ruled Annan; it was not until the 1300s that Islamization caused a shift to Arabic-derived scripts in the Malay world. From the sixth to tenth centuries, the Eurasian steppe was predominantly Turkic in language and culture, with significant Iranian influences introduced by the Sogdians (e.g., Manichaeism), and its khaganates typically used Sogdian writing or the Sogdian-derived Old Turkic script. Until the ninth century, Central Asia used a variety of Indic and Iranian scripts, with Sogdian serving as a spoken lingua franca.[215] However, the Sogdian language would die out in Islamic Central Asia during the tenth and eleventh centuries because of competition from another Iranian language,

[213] Backus, *The Nan-chao Kingdom*, 86–87.
[214] Takata, "A Note on the Lijiang Tibetan Inscription."
[215] See Chin, "Colonization, Sinicization, and the Polyscriptic Northwest."

Persian. A Muslim dynasty of Iranian origin, the Samanids, ruled over Khurasan, Sogdiana, and Fergana in the ninth and tenth centuries, and promoted a new courtly culture in which New Persian, written with the Arabic script rather than Pahlavi, served as the language of elite writing.[216] The Samanids fell in the 990s to the Turkic Karakhanids, who had themselves converted to Islam in 934. Under Karakhanid rule, Persian-speaking Muslim Sogdians and Ferganans adopted a new identity as *Tajik*, a Persian term once used to refer primarily to Arab Muslims.[217]

Because the Tang only sent soldiers, not permanent colonists, to the Tarim and Dzungarian basins between the 640s and 760s, there is no evidence of linguistic change in Central Asia caused by Tang influence. Despite more than a century of continuous Tang military occupation under the Anxi Protectorate (692–ca. 800), the Tarim Basin did not truly become a part of the Sinographic sphere: Khotanese literature, for example, was written in Brahmi script and heavily influenced by Sanskrit Buddhist texts, rather than texts in Literary Sinitic. Sinographic civilization did not spread further west than Gaochang (Turfan), which itself was already part of the Sinographic sphere long before its annexation by the Tang in 640. Gaochang's local elite was descended from Han-era colonists who had displaced the original Tocharian language with Literary Sinitic culture, leading the Sogdians (who also had a large immigrant community there) to give its capital a name that translates as "Chinatown."[218] The Tang garrisons in the Tarim and Dzungarian basins appear to have been fully assimilated into the local populations after the eighth century, leaving no cultural impact. In contrast, the ninth-century Uighur migration to the Tarim Basin caused the permanent displacement of the Tocharian languages of Agni and Kucha by Old Uighur, written in the Sogdian-derived Old Uighur alphabet. The Saka Iranian languages of *Shulik (Shule, Kashgar) and Khotan similarly disappeared under Karakhanid rule in the tenth and eleventh centuries, replaced by Karluk Middle Turkic.[219] Gaochang remained semi-Sinographic into the thirteenth century, but developed a unique mix of Sinitic, Turkic, and Sogdian cultures as the capital of a Uighur state that extended north to Beshbalik and west to Kucha.[220]

---

[216] Other Turkic dynasties that emerged from the Samanid realm, namely the Ghaznavids and Seljuks, spread the new Persianate elite culture to Afghanistan and Iran, creating a cultural sphere that some scholars now call (with inspiration from Pollock) the Persian cosmopolis. Tor, "The Islamization of Central Asia"; Green, "The Frontiers of the Persianate World."

[217] The Middle Persian form *tāzīk* was the root of *Dashi* (Middle Chinese *Dazhik*), the Tang name for the Arabs.

[218] Hansen, *The Silk Road*, 141.

[219] The Karakhanids are said to have captured Shulik in 934–55 and Khotan in 1006.

[220] On this state, the rulers of which were originally Manichaean but eventually switched to Buddhism, see Kasai, "Uyghur Legitimation and the Role of Buddhism."

The period of Tibetan rule in Gansu (760s–840s) resulted in a multicultural and multilingual environment in which Tibetan officials and troops governed with the assistance of local Chinese and Sogdian elite families, whose members adopted Tibetan names and became fluent in Tibetan. Non-elite Chinese in Dunhuang even learned to use the Tibetan script to write Sinitic, thus avoiding having to master Sinographic literacy.[221] Although irredentists among the Chang'an elite frequently claimed that the Gansu Chinese were struggling to resist cultural Tibetanization while longing for a liberating Tang army, the end of Tibetan rule did not translate into a "re-Sinicization" of the region. As mentioned earlier, Wuzong's court had planned a full reconquest of Gansu and eastern Qinghai after the Tibetan empire's collapse, but the actual reconquest undertaken by his successor in 849 was limited to a narrow strip of territory stretching through Ningxia, Gansu, and Sichuan. The court then got distracted by a Tangut revolt in the Ordos and decided not to expend further resources on the irredentist project, especially after a warlord state founded by the Chinese Zhang family of Dunhuang captured most of the Gansu Corridor and formally submitted to Tang suzerainty.[222] The Tang court dubbed this Chinese-ruled regime the Guiyi ("Return to Allegiance") Command. It remained effectively independent but lost most of its territory to Uighur refugees in the 870s and 880s, though it held on to Dunhuang and the adjacent prefecture of Guazhou until the 1030s. Meanwhile, Qinghai and most of southern Gansu (extending north to Liangzhou) remained divided between Tibetan warlords and bands of Tibetan or Tibetanized former slave-soldiers; descendants of Tang subjects in these areas eventually assimilated to a Tibetan identity.[223] The result of these geopolitical shifts was that the Sinographic sphere had mostly retreated from Gansu by the beginning of the tenth century, except for a small Sinographic but semi-Tibetanized state in Dunhuang-Guazhou, sandwiched between the Uighur states of Gaochang and Ganzhou (Zhangye, Gansu). After the tenth century, Uighur displaced Sinitic, Sogdian, and Tibetan as the primary written and spoken language in even Dunhuang.[224]

The Tang court's half-hearted effort toward reclaiming the lost northwestern frontier may have something to do with the late Tang literati's embrace of the self-comforting position that the empire could still "win" culturally where it had failed to conquer militarily. Naturally, they cited the Sinographic sphere as proof of this. In the mid-ninth century, for example, Sun Qiao (fl. 838–85) composed an essay that interpreted the extension of Literary Sinitic education to

---

[221] Takata, "Tibetan Dominion over Dunhuang."   [222] *ZZTJ* 248.8036–41, 249.8043–49.

[223] Yang, *Frontiers of the Tang and Song Empires*, Map 7, at https://storymaps.arcgis.com/stories/0cf798878745406fa5719b97ccfc5454#ref-n-2tAtnW; Yang, "Stubbornly Chinese?"

[224] Takata, "Multilingualism in Tun-huang."

Silla and Nanzhao as evidence of the Tang dynasty's greatness. The essay is notable for its ethnocentric, condescending, and dehumanizing rhetoric regarding the "barbarian" peoples purportedly civilized by Chinese influence:

> To the east of Qi [Shandong], who knows how many thousands of *li* across the great sea, lies the biggest country of the island barbarians, called Silla. To the south of Shu [Sichuan], past Kunming and 7,000 to 8,000 *li* across uncultivated lands, lies the strongest country of the Man barbarians, called Nanzhao. These are both bird-like and beast-like peoples whose unintelligible languages sound like the screeching of shrikes. They dress in animal skins and are violent and fierce. It is difficult to transform their long-entrenched customs.
>
> But since the Tang began ruling the realm [*tianxia*, "All Under Heaven"], the people of these two countries have all put Confucian teachings first and have come to resemble the Chinese [Xia] people in civility and refinement. Among the great clans of Silla, some have even produced men who studied in our superior state and took the civil service examinations, winning fame alongside our ministers' sons. They are using books to a previously unheard-of extent. They were born in distant seas or miasmic wastelands and knew only of archery and horsemanship, of warfare and hunting. What did they know of literary arts and Confucian learning? But now they have changed their bestial hearts and understand ritual etiquette. They have stopped folding their robes to the left and now dress like we do.[225] Is this not due to the far-reaching wind of our emperors' influence?
>
> I have heard that wherever civilizing influence extends, even the trees and rocks and animals know how to turn to its moral charisma. For that reason, auspicious omens will appear, such as men with unusual talents and strange appearances. The two countries [Silla and Nanzhao] are auspicious omens, and such omens never occur singly. There will surely be more of their kind; surely, lands across the eastern sea and peoples that have never submitted will turn to our influence and be transformed![226]

In another essay from the 850s, however, Sun Qiao expressed a much less triumphalist perspective on Nanzhao's advancement into the rank of "civilized" states. This piece is framed as an interview with Tian Zaibin, a general with three years' experience as a prefect on the Sichuan frontier. Tian quotes a saying that has become common in Sichuan: "The western barbarians (i.e., Tibetans) we could still take, but the southern barbarians (i.e., Nanzhao) will be the death of us!" He claims that Wei Gao's educational program has ultimately proven ruinous to Sichuan's people, as the experience of studying in Chengdu has given hundreds of Nanzhao aristocrats an intimate knowledge of the province's strategic geography. Nanzhao has already used this knowledge once to raid

---

[225] Chinese one-piece robes typically folded and fastened on the right, except in the case of robes worn by the dead during funerary rites. In contrast, "barbarian" peoples were believed to fold their robes to the left, the *locus classicus* for this being Confucius's words in *Analects* 14.17.

[226] *QTW* Chapter 794.

and sack Chengdu in 829, taking large amounts of loot and livestock and tens of thousands of Chinese captives. And that is not the end of it, Tian warns: "Ever since then, the Man barbarians have often thought of massacring Shu [Sichuan]. At home, they multiply their livestock and accumulate their grain; on the border, they train their troops and study military tactics."[227]

Tian Zaibin's fears were not unfounded, though Nanzhao was not solely to blame for its tensions with the Tang. In fact, Nanzhao mended fences with the Tang after 829, returning some 4,000 of its Chinese captives, and then turned its attention to invading its southern neighbors, the Pyu states of Burma.[228] But Tang officials in Sichuan eventually grew weary of the costs of the Chengdu educational program and of hosting the increasingly large tribute missions that Nanzhao sent to the Tang court – presumably aimed at receiving more imperial largesse in return.[229] Perhaps, after the sudden collapse of the Tibetan empire in the 840s, good relations with Nanzhao were no longer viewed as a priority worth investing in. In the 850s, new limits were placed on the size of student cohorts and embassies from Nanzhao; King Quanfengyou (r. 823–59) then angrily ended his participation in the educational program, ceased sending tribute to Chang'an, and began raiding the Sichuan frontier again.[230]

Things came to a head in 859 when the new Tang emperor Yizong declined to issue an edict of investiture to Quanfengyou's successor Shilong (r. 859–77), on the grounds that his name violated official taboos on the names of Taizong and Xuanzong. In response, Shilong declared himself an emperor, renamed his state as Dali, and seized the Tang prefecture of Bozhou (Zunyi, Guizhou), effectively challenging the Tang to a showdown.[231] In the ensuing conflict, the last major war that the Tang fought with a foreign power, Dali troops twice captured Hanoi (seat of the Annan protectorate) and repeatedly attacked Chengdu, aided by Man and Lao tribes who resented abuses suffered at the hands of venal Tang frontier administrators.[232] Tang armies in Annan and Sichuan, reinforced by units mobilized from provinces across the empire, managed to avoid permanent territorial losses but never attempted a counteroffensive into Dali territory, perhaps due to lingering memories of the disastrous invasions of Nanzhao more than a century earlier. The Tang–Dali war lasted twenty years (860–80), outlasting the reigns of

---

[227] *QTW* Chapter 795. On the 829 sack of Chengdu, see also the detailed analysis in Backus, *The Nan-chao Kingdom*, 105–22.

[228] Backus, *The Nan-chao Kingdom*, 126–30.   [229] *ZZTJ* 249.8078.   [230] Ibid.

[231] Ibid. The Tang retook Bozhou in 860 but soon lost it again. The local Yang family, probably of indigenous "Man" origin, seized control of the prefecture in 876 and ruled it as an autonomous state for over seven centuries, until the Ming dynasty annexed it in 1600.

[232] Backus, *The Nan-chao Kingdom*, 131–53; Yang, *Frontiers of the Tang and Song Empires*, Map 7, at https://storymaps.arcgis.com/stories/0cf798878745406fa5719b97ccfc5454#ref-n-2tAtnW.

both Yizong and Shilong, and exacted a huge cost in wealth and manpower on both sides. In 880, after much debate, the Tang court reluctantly agreed to a peace settlement that included significant concessions to Dali: formal diplomatic parity in the form of fictive brotherhood, and marriage between a Tang imperial princess (Yizong's daughter Princess Anhua) and Shilong's successor Longshun (r. 877–97).[233] Some ministers objected vehemently to granting such privileges to a "barbarian" state as small as Dali, insisting that the dynasty's prestige was at stake. But others argued, more persuasively, that with the dynasty now broke and on the verge of internal collapse from the Huang Chao Rebellion, survival outweighed prestige in importance.[234]

The Tang–Dali war shows that while foreign relations within the Sinographic sphere were generally more peaceful in the ninth century than in the seventh, they were not conflict-free. A state's incorporation into the Sinographic sphere did not mean unconditional acceptance of Chinese supremacy at the expense of its own interests, any more than participating in the tributary system served as a guarantee of security from Chinese aggression. As Sinographic states, Nanzhao/Dali, Silla, Bohai, and Japan benefited from using the Chinese textual tradition as a source for models with which to centralize their institutions, systematize their laws, enhance their legitimacy and prestige, and create literate aristocratic cultures. But these states also learned to play the game of geopolitics skillfully to preserve their freedom of action, or simply to survive despite being significantly smaller and weaker than neighboring empires.

- Nanzhao first protected its sovereignty by playing the Tang and Tibetan empires against each other. After the Tibetan empire's collapse removed the danger of being attacked by both powers at once, the kings of Nanzhao soon began constructing their own imperial polity (Dali) using a combination of Sinitic, Esoteric Buddhist, and Southeast Asian political cultures.[235]
- While paying tribute to the Tang, Bohai and Japan developed a close diplomatic and trading relationship in which Bohai's king accepted vassalage to the Japanese emperor, allowing Japan to construct a miniature tributary system of its own.[236]

---

[233] Backus, *The Nan-chao Kingdom*, 153–58. Princess Anhua's marriage to Longshun was disrupted by Huang Chao's capture of Chang'an in early 881 and the Tang court's flight to Sichuan, leading to some confusion over whether it ever took place at all (e.g., Backus argues, based on the *Xin Tangshu*, that it did not). Recent research shows, however, that it's likely the princess did finally arrive in Nanzhao: Du, "Tang Anhua zhang gongzhu."

[234] *ZZTJ* 253.8204, 8227–28.

[235] Bryson, "Tsenpo Chung, Yunnan Wang, Mahārāja"; Daniels, "Nanzhao as a Southeast Asian kingdom."

[236] On Bohai–Japan relations, with an emphasis on the importance of Literary Sinitic poetry in their diplomatic interactions, see Morley, "Poetry and Diplomacy in Early Heian Japan."

- After driving the Tang out of the Korean peninsula, Silla reverted to cultivating strong tributary relations with the Chinese court to strengthen the royal house's authority over the true-bone nobles and to offset the Bohai–Japan alliance. Silla subtly resisted Japan's attempts at treating it as a vassal rather than an equal, while maintaining a northern buffer zone to avoid direct conflict with both Bohai and the Tang.[237]

Acknowledging the agency and legitimate interests of these minor states would allow us to write a less Sinocentric narrative of East Asia's history in this period, one that doesn't treat Tang hegemony as normative or narrate its diminution in the eighth and ninth centuries as a sad tale of imperial decline.

Conclusion: The Fall of the Tang in East Asian History

In the last thirty years of its history, the Tang empire was rocked by a massive peasant rebellion and then disintegrated into a patchwork of warlord states. Historians continue to investigate the causes of this collapse. Song dynasty historians tended to argue that the costs of the war with Dali had bled the imperial treasury dry and overburdened the populace with heavy taxes, driving the peasants to breaking point in a repeat of the Sui dynasty's fall.[238] Both Song and modern historians have also blamed Emperor Xizong (Li Xuan, r. 873–88), who ascended the throne aged eleven and neglected to deal with his empire's escalating crisis while indulging his interests and talents in horse archery, swordsmanship, mathematics, music, kickball, cockfighting, gambling, and especially polo (he reportedly boasted that if the examinations were based on polo, he would take first place).[239] Less often recognized is the responsibility borne by Xizong's father Yizong, whose extravagant spending and negligence sowed the seeds for the empire's rapid decline after his death. Even at the height of the Dali war in 869–70, and with a rebellion raging in the Jiangsu region, Yizong spent huge amounts of the imperial state's wealth on a wedding for his favorite daughter, followed by an equally extravagant funeral when she died a year later. He also lavished donations on the Buddhist *sangha*, including the Famen Temple, while indulging in banqueting and delegating policymaking to ministers known to be extremely corrupt.[240] The record of Yizong's reign shows that the biggest problem facing the Tang court at this time was not a lack of

---

[237] Choi, "Silla's Perception of the International World Order"; Kim, "A Buffer Zone for Peace."
[238] *XTS* 222b.6292, 6295, 222c.6332–33.   [239] *ZZTJ* 253.8221.
[240] *ZZTJ* 251.8139, 8150, 252.8161–62, 8165. Yizong's extravagance can still be glimpsed from the exquisite gold and silver objects that he gifted to the Famen Temple in 873; these were rediscovered in the temple's crypt in 1987.

resources, but rather sheer waste and mismanagement of the still-plentiful resources it had at its disposal.

By the time Xizong's reign began, the North China Plain had suffered years of drought and famine in succession.[241] One of Xizong's ministers persuaded him to exempt the affected regions from taxation, but local authorities apparently ignored the order and continued pressing the peasants mercilessly for taxes. Without adequate relief efforts by the state, starving peasants formed bands of refugees and took to banditry to survive. Local officials covered up the magnitude of the rural distress to protect themselves from blame, so the imperial court did not effectively mobilize either famine relief or military suppression until the bandit groups had grown into large rebel armies.[242] These armies were led by Wang Xianzhi (d. 878) and Huang Chao (835–84), whose families had previously prospered by trafficking salt outside the state monopoly. Although Tang armies defeated and killed Wang Xianzhi in 878, years of wasteful spending, drought, locust plagues, and warfare against both the rebels and Dali had by then drained the government of all its reserves. As tax collection was no longer feasible in many parts of the empire, the state was forced to borrow cash and grain from merchants and rich landlords and sell political sinecures to pay its officials and troops.[243] In 878–81, Huang Chao led his army on a rampage through south China and then, when the court refused his demand to be made a provincial governor, marched north and captured both Luoyang and Chang'an from underprepared and demoralized imperial troops (Figure 7). Xizong escaped to Sichuan, but most of the imperial clan, as well as hundreds of court officials and their families, were trapped in Chang'an and slaughtered by vengeful rebels who blamed them for the peasantry's misery.[244]

Huang Chao founded his own imperial dynasty in Chang'an but was driven out, hunted down, and killed by the Shatuo Türks in 883 – once again, Turkic cavalry had come to the Tang's rescue.[245] Xizong returned to his desolate capital, much as Suzong had done in 757; but this time, the damage done to

---

[241] Historians and paleoclimatologists are still debating whether these were part of a global phase of climate change that also caused the collapse of the Uighur khaganate, Silla, and the Classic Maya civilization. See Fan, "Climatic Change and Dynastic Cycles in Chinese History"; Anderson, *The East Asian World-System*, 129, 134–35. Anderson's book is an original, ambitious effort at identifying cyclical patterns in East Asian and world history and relating them to climatic change and world-systems theory. But his treatment of the Tang period is significantly weakened by reliance on dated and inaccurate secondary sources. To his credit, however, he heeds Fan's caution regarding climatic determinism in interpreting the fall of the Tang.

[242] *ZZTJ* 251.8144–45, 8168–69, 8174, 8180.   [243] *ZZTJ* 253.8203.

[244] On the fall of Chang'an and ensuing violence against the capital elite, see Tackett, *The Destruction of the Medieval Chinese Aristocracy*, 189–200.

[245] In fact, the Shatuo leader Li Keyong (856–908) had himself only recently been in open revolt against the Tang court but seized this chance to get back in the dynasty's good graces.

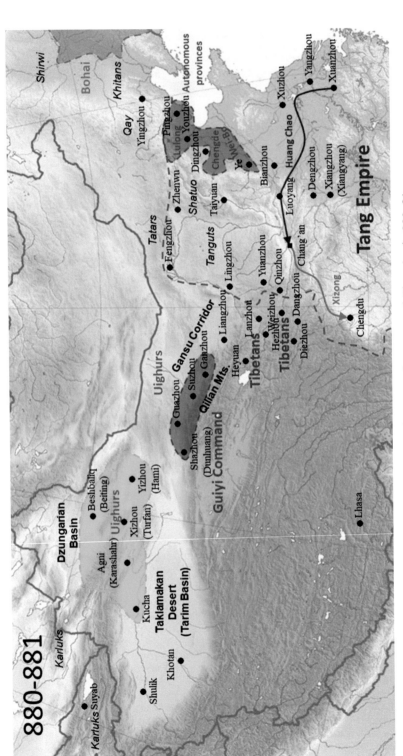

Figure 7 Map of Huang Chao's advance on Luoyang and Chang'an in 880–81

the imperial court's authority was irreversible. For the next two decades, the increasingly dysfunctional and factionalized court failed to restore order to an empire divided between many warlords, most of them rogue provincial governors or former rebels. Most regions of both north and south China were devastated by warlord conflicts, even if they had previously been spared the rebels' depredations.[246]

In 903, the warlord Zhu Wen (852–912) seized control over the court of Emperor Zhaozong (Li Ye, r. 888–904). Zhu had Zhaozong murdered a year later and replaced with an eleven-year-old prince. In 907 Zhu, having tired of ruling through a puppet, usurped the throne and founded the Liang dynasty (907–23). The Shatuo, identifying as both loyalists and heirs to the defunct Tang, built a strong rival state in Shanxi and conquered the Liang in 923. From then until 951, three short-lived Shatuo military dynasties (known to historians as Later Tang, Later Jin, and Later Han) successively ruled north China. South China remained divided between other warlord regimes and would not be reunified with the north until the 970s. Reunification took place under the ethnically Chinese Song dynasty, founded by a military family that achieved a lasting restoration of stable, centralized civil governance; the most historically significant innovation in this regard was an expanded and more meritocratic examination system that replaced older patron-client networks and gave southern literati families greater access to political office.[247] Also built into the Song political system were institutional norms favoring the educated literati and preventing military men from holding political power. Perhaps due in part to this systemic disempowerment of both Chinese and Inner Asian military families, the Shatuo were the last Turkic military elite to play a significant role in Chinese political history.[248] In contrast, the westward migration of numerous Turkic-speaking steppe peoples and the employment of many Turks as elite slave-soldiers in the Abbasid realm gave them influence in the politics of the Islamic world for centuries to come, culminating in the Mamluk Sultanate of Egypt and the Ottoman Empire.

The decline and fall of the Tang created political opportunities for other peoples on the empire's periphery who had previously lived in the shadow of Chinese domination. Dali, having fulfilled its ambition of becoming a bona fide imperial state, went through its own period of political turmoil in the early

---

[246] Tackett, *The Destruction of the Medieval Chinese Aristocracy*, 200–30.

[247] The classic study of the Song civil service examinations is Chaffee, *The Thorny Gates of Learning*.

[248] The Shatuo appear to have assimilated relatively quickly into the Chinese population during the early Song period, though this process is unfortunately entirely invisible in the extant sources.

900s but reemerged under the capable management of the Duan family, who would rule Yunnan as emperors from 937 to 1253.[249] The province of Annan broke away from the Chinese warlord state in Guangdong during the 930s and, after a period of division known as the Twelve Warlords (944–68), was united into an enduring independent polity.[250] This Đại Việt state eventually expanded southward into the lands of the Austronesian-speaking Cham people (Champa) and laid the foundations for a Vietnamese national identity. For leading troops against Huang Chao after the fall of Chang'an, a Tangut family was rewarded with hereditary governorship of the Ordos region and used this as a basis to build the Xia state in the tenth century. Xia (also known as Xi Xia or Western Xia) successfully resisted incorporation by the Song and conquered the Gansu Corridor and parts of eastern Qinghai, ruling over a polyglot population of Tanguts, Uighurs, Tibetans, and Chinese. But the biggest success story was that of the Khitans, who united their tribes into a powerful empire (the Liao) that conquered Bohai (926), annexed the northernmost prefectures in Hebei and Shanxi (936–8), briefly occupied the North China Plain (947), gained overlordship over Goryeo (993), and finally achieved formal diplomatic parity with the Song dynasty (1005), under peace terms that included generous annual subsidies of silk and silver from the Song.[251] Although the Khitans did not fully incorporate the Mongolian steppe into their imperial state, they asserted suzerainty over its tribes via demands for tribute and periodic punitive expeditions, which are believed to have driven yet more Turkic tribes westward into Central Asia and contributed to Mongolia becoming primarily Mongolic-speaking.[252] The role formerly played by the Tang, of an empire straddling East Asia and Inner Asia, was therefore now played by the Liao and not the Song.

Dali, Đại Việt, Xia, and Liao all had Sinographic elites, though the Khitan and Tangut elites also created new writing systems for their own languages, loosely modeled on Sinographic writing.[253] All four states adopted bureaucratic institutions adapted from the Tang model. All four had elites as fervently Buddhist as the Tang elite had been, although Dali and Xia (being contiguous with both the Sinitic and Tibetan worlds) displayed a preference for Esoteric

[249] Backus, *The Nan-chao Kingdom*, 160–64.   [250] See Taylor, *The Birth of Vietnam*.

[251] Recent scholarship on the Xia and Liao is extensive, but I especially recommend two articles on their imperial ideologies: Solonin, "The Formation of Tangut Ideology"; Xue, "Age of Emperors." For digital maps of the Song-Liao and Song-Xia borders, see Yang, *Frontiers of the Tang and Song Empires*, Map 10 and Map 11, at https://storymaps.arcgis.com/stories/ 0cf798878745406fa5719b97ccfc5454#ref-n-pZ6zFE and https://storymaps.arcgis.com/stor ies/0cf798878745406fa5719b97ccfc5454#ref-n-bYPaUu.

[252] Biran, "Unearthing the Liao Dynasty's Relations with the Muslim World," 226–27.

[253] The literate elites of Dali and Đại Việt transcribed their language using Sinographs but also created numerous new Sinographs for this purpose.

Buddhism with roots in both Tang and Tibetan traditions.[254] Together with the Song, Goryeo, and Japan, these states formed an enlarged Sinographic sphere characterized by the geopolitical and cultural legacy of the Tang empire. The Khitan Liao fell to its eastern vassals, the Jurchen people, in the 1120s, but the Jurchens (descendants of the Amur River Margat) were themselves able to build a Sinographic empire at an accelerated pace by employing former Liao officials and adopting Liao institutions. They then swiftly overpowered the Song dynasty and conquered north China, fusing Manchuria and the Sinitic heartland into a single empire for the first time in history. Meanwhile, a faction of the Khitan elite evaded the Jurchen conquest by migrating to Central Asia, where they gained suzerainty over the Karakhanids and established a new empire in an unprecedented merging of the Sinographic and Turco-Islamic worlds.[255] Those worlds would merge on a much larger scale in the thirteenth century under the Mongol empire, which straddled Inner Asia and East Asia to an extent that neither the Tang nor the Liao could have thought possible. Nevertheless, the multilingual and polycentric but culturally interconnected East Asian region that the Mongols encountered and invaded was both a product of the Tang empire's efforts at drawing surrounding polities into its orbit, and a testimony to some of those polities' subsequent success in making their own history as imperial states.

---

[254] Sørensen, "Esoteric Buddhism in the Nanzhao and Dali Kingdoms"; Dunnell, "Esoteric Buddhism under the Xixia."

[255] Biran, *The Empire of the Qara Khitai.*

Abbreviations

ALS: Yao Runeng 姚汝能, *An Lushan shiji* 安祿山事迹 [Biography of An Lushan] (Beijing: Zhonghua shuju, 2006).

CFYG: Wang Qinruo 王欽若 *et al.*, *Cefu yuangui* 冊府元龜 [Outstanding Models from the Storehouse of Literature] (Nanjing: Fenghuang chubanshe, 2006).

JTS: Liu Xu 劉煦 *et al.*, *Jiu Tangshu* 舊唐書 [Old History of the Tang] (Beijing: Zhonghua shuju, 1975).

QTW: Dong Gao 董誥, *Quan Tangwen* 全唐文 [Complete Anthology of Tang Prose] (Beijing: Zhonghua shuju, 1983).

TD: Du You 杜佑, *Tongdian* 通典 [Comprehensive Institutions] (Beijing: Zhonghua shuju, 1988).

THY: Wang Pu 王溥, *Tang huiyao* 唐會要 [Institutional History of the Tang] (Taipei: Shijie shuju, 1968).

TLSY: Zhangsun Wuji 長孫無忌 *et al.*, *Tanglü shuyi* 唐律疏議 [The Tang Code with Commentaries] (Beijing: Zhonghua shuju, 1983).

XTS: Ouyang Xiu 歐陽修 *et al.*, *Xin Tangshu* 新唐書 [New History of the Tang] (Beijing: Zhonghua shuju, 1975).

ZZTJ: Sima Guang 司馬光 *et al.*, *Zizhi tongjian* 資治通鑑 [Comprehensive Mirror to Aid Governance] (Beijing: Zhonghua shuju, 1956).

Bibliography

Abramson, Marc S. *Ethnic Identity in Tang China* (Philadelphia: University of Pennsylvania Press, 2008).

Akin, Alexander. "The *Jing Xing Ji* of Du Huan: Notes on the West by a Chinese Prisoner of War," *Harvard Middle Eastern and Islamic Review* 5 (1999–2000), 77–102.

al-Sirafi, Abu Zayd (trans. Tim Mackintosh-Smith). *Accounts of China and India* (New York: New York University Press, 2017).

Anderson, Eugene N. *The East Asian World-System: Climate and Dynastic Change* (Cham: Springer, 2019).

Backus, Charles. *The Nan-chao Kingdom and T'ang China's Southwestern Frontier* (Cambridge: Cambridge University Press, 1981).

Baghbibi, Hassan Rezai. "New Light on the Middle Persian-Chinese Bilingual Inscription from Xi'an," in *The Persian Language in History*, eds. Mauro Maggi and Paola Orsatti (Wiesbaden: Dr. Ludwig Reichert Verlag, 2011), 105–15.

Barenghi, Maddalena. "The Making of the Shatuo: Military Leadership and Border Unrest in North China's Daibei (808–880)," *Central Asiatic Journal*, 63.1–2 (2020), 39–70.

Barenghi, Maddalena. "Representations of Descent: Origin and Migration Stories of the Ninth- and Tenth-Century Turkic Shatuo," *Asia Major* 32.1 (2019), 53–86.

Beckwith, Christopher I. *The Tibetan Empire in Central Asia* (Princeton, NJ: Princeton University Press, 1987).

Bi Bo 畢波, "Daluosi zhi zhan he Tianwei jian'er fu Suiye" 怛羅斯之戰和天威健兒赴碎葉 [The Battle of Talas and the Deployment of Troops from the Tianwei Garrison to Suyab], *Lishi yanjiu* 歷史研究 2 (2007), 15–24.

Bi Bo 畢波. *Zhonggu Zhongguo de Sute Huren – yi Chang'an wei zhongxin* 中古中國的粟特胡人 – 以長安爲中心 [Sogdians in Medieval China: With Special Reference to the Sogdian Presence in the Capital Chang'an] (Zhongguo renmin daxue chubanshe, 2011).

Biran, Michal. *The Empire of the Qara Khitai in Eurasian History: Between China and the Islamic World* (Cambridge: Cambridge University Press, 2005).

Biran, Michal. "Unearthing the Liao Dynasty's Relations with the Muslim World: Migrations, Diplomacy, Commerce, and Mutual Perceptions," *Journal of Song-Yuan Studies* 43 (2013), 221–51.

Bloom, Jonathan. *Paper before Print: The History and Impact of Paper in the Islamic World* (New Haven, CT: Yale University Press, 2001).

Brose, Benjamin. *Patrons and Patriarchs: Regional Rulers and Chan Monks during the Five Dynasties and Ten Kingdoms* (Honolulu: University of Hawaii Press, 2015).

Bryson, Megan. "Tsenpo Chung, Yunnan Wang, Mahārāja: Royal Titles in Narratives of Nanzhao Kingship between Tibet and Tang China," *Cahiers D'Extrême-Asie* 24 (2015), 59–76.

Chaffee, John W. *The Muslim Merchants of Premodern China: The History of a Maritime Asian Trade Diaspora, 750–1400* (Cambridge: Cambridge University Press, 2018).

Chaffee, John W. *The Thorny Gates of Learning in Sung China: A Social History of Examinations* (Albany, NY: SUNY Press, 1995).

Chen Chong 陳翀. "Hui'e dongchuan 'Baishi wenji' ji Putuo Luojia kaishan kao" 慧萼東傳《白氏文集》及普陀洛迦開山考 [A Study of Egaku's Transmission of "Mister Bai's Collected Works" to the East and the Establishment of the First Temple on Fudarakusan], *Zhejiang daxue xuebao* 浙江大學學報 8 (2010), 1–11.

Chen, Fan-Pen. "Problems of Chinese Historiography As Seen in the Official Records on Yang Kuei-fei," *T'ang Studies* 8–9 (1990–1), 83–96.

Chen, Jinhua. "A Chinese Monk under a 'Barbarian' Mask? Zhihuilun (?–876) and Late Tang Esoteric Buddhism," *T'oung Pao* 99.1–3 (2013), 88–139.

Chen Ken 陳懇. "Chile yu Tiele zuming xinzheng" 敕勒與鐵勒族名新證 [New Evidence on the Ethnonyms Chile and Tiele], *International Journal of Eurasian Studies* (*Ouya xuekan* 歐亞學刊) 11 (2022), 59–88.

Ch'en, Kenneth. "The Economic Background of The Hui-ch'ang Suppression of Buddhism," *Harvard Journal of Asiatic Studies* 19.1–2 (1956), 67–105.

Chin, Tamara T. "Colonization, Sinicization, and the Polyscriptic Northwest," in *The Oxford Handbook of Classical Chinese Literature*, eds. Wiebke Denecke, Wai-Yee Li, and Xiaofei Tian (Oxford: Oxford University Press, 2017), 487–92.

Chittick, Andrew. *The Jiankang Empire in Chinese and World History* (Oxford: Oxford University Press, 2020).

Choi, Heejoon. "Silla's Perception of the International World Order As Seen through Diplomatic Documents," *International Journal of Korean History* 24.2 (2019), 171–205.

Dang Yinping 黨銀平. *Tang yu Xinluo wenhua guanxi yanjiu* 唐與新羅文化關係研究 [Studies on the Cultural Relations between the Tang and Silla] (Beijing: Zhonghua shuju, 2008).

Daniels, Christian. "Nanzhao As a Southeast Asian Kingdom, c.738–902," *Journal of Southeast Asian Studies* 52.2 (2021), 188–213.

Denecke, Wiebke and Nam Nguyen. "Shared Literary Heritage in the East Asian Sinographic Sphere," in *The Oxford Handbook of Classical Chinese Literature*, eds. Wiebke Denecke, Wai-Yee Li, and Xiaofei Tian (Oxford: Oxford University Press, 2017), 510–32.

Di Cosmo, Nicola. "Maligned Exchanges: The Uyghur-Tang Trade in the Light of Climate Data," in *Texts and Transformations: Essays in Honor of the 75th Birthday of Victor H. Mair*, ed. Haun Saussy (Amherst, NY: Cambria Press, 2018), 117–36.

Dong Chunlin 董春林. "An-Shi zhi luan hou Hexi Tiele buzu de qianxi – yi Tangdai Qibi zu wei li" 安史之亂後河西鐵勒部族的遷徙 – 以唐代契苾族爲例 [The Migration of the Tegreg Tribes of Hexi after the An Lushan Rebellion – Using the Kibir Tribe in the Tang As an Example], *Qinghai minzu daxue xuebao* 青海民族大學學報 38.1 (2012), 81–84.

Dotson, Brandon. *The Old Tibetan Annals: An Annotated Translation of Tibet's First History* (Vienna: Verlag der osterreichischen Akademie der Wissenschaften, 2009).

Drompp, Michael R. *Tang China and the Collapse of the Uighur Empire: A Documentary History* (Leiden: Brill, 2005).

Du Chenghui 杜成輝. "Tang Anhua zhang gongzhu Nanzhao heqin kao" 唐安化長公主南詔和亲考 [A Study of the Tang Princess Anhua's Marriage to the King of Nanzhao], *Dali xueyuan xuebao* 大理學院學報 8.3 (2009), 1–4.

Dunnell, Ruth. "Esoteric Buddhism under the Xixia (1038–1227)," in *Esoteric Buddhism and the Tantras in East Asia*, eds. Charles D. Orzech, Henrik H. Sorensen, and Richard K. Payne (Leiden: Brill, 2011), 465–77.

El-Hibri, Tayeb. *The Abbasid Caliphate: A History* (Cambridge: Cambridge University Press, 2021).

Fan, Ka-wai. "Climatic Change and Dynastic Cycles in Chinese History: A Review Essay," *Climatic Change* 101 (2010), 565–73.

Fang Xuanling 房玄齡 et al. *Jinshu* 晉書 [History of the Jin] (Beijing: Zhonghua shuju, 1974).

Forte, Antonino. *The Hostage An Shigao and His Offspring: An Iranian Family in China* (Kyoto: Italian School of East Asian Studies, 1995).

Forte, Antonino. "Iranians in China: Buddhism, Zoroastrianism, and Bureaus of Commerce," *Cahiers D'Extrême-Asie* 11 (1999), 277–90.

Forte, Antonino. "Kuwabara's Misleading Thesis on Bukhara and the Family Name An," *Journal of the American Oriental Society* 116.4 (1996), 645–52.

Fu Lo-ch'eng (Fu Lecheng) 傅樂成. *Han Tang shilun ji* 漢唐史論集 [Collected Essays on the History of the Han and Tang] (Taipei: Lianjing, 1977).

George, Alain. "Direct Sea Trade between Early Islamic Iraq and Tang China: From the Exchange of Goods to the Transmission of Ideas," *Journal of the Royal Asiatic Society, Series 3*, 25.4 (2015), 579–624.

Goble, Geoffrey C. *Chinese Esoteric Buddhism: Amoghavajra, the Ruling Elite, and the Emergence of a Tradition* (New York: Columbia University Press, 2019).

Graff, David A. *Medieval Chinese Warfare, 300–900* (London: Routledge, 2002).

Green, Nile. "The Frontiers of the Persianate World (ca. 800–1900)," in *The Persianate World: The Frontiers of a Eurasian Lingua Franca*, ed. Nile Green (Berkeley: University of California Press, 2019), 9–17.

Gulácsi, Zsuzsanna. "A Manichaean 'Portrait of the Buddha Jesus': Identifying a Twelfth- or Thirteenth-Century Chinese Painting from the Collection of Seiun-Ji Zen Temple," *Artibus Asiae* 69.1 (2009), 91–145.

Haug, Robert. *The Eastern Frontier: Limits of Empire in Late Antique and Early Medieval Central Asia* (London: I. B. Tauris, 2019).

Heng, Derek. *Southeast Asian Interactions: Geography, Networks, and Trade*, Elements in the Global Middle Ages (Cambridge: Cambridge University Press, 2022).

Heng, Derek. "The Tang Shipwreck and the Nature of China's Maritime Trade during the Late Tang Period," in *The Tang Shipwreck: Art and Exchange in the 9th Century*, eds. Alan Chong and Stephen A. Murphy (Singapore: Asian Civilizations Museum, 2019), 142–59.

Heng, Geraldine. "An Ordinary Ship and Its Stories of Early Globalism: World Travel, Mass Production, and Art in the Global Middle Ages," *Journal of Medieval Worlds* 1.1 (2019), 11–54.

Hua Tao. "Central and Western Tianshan on the Eve of Islamization," *Journal of Asian History* 27.2 (1993), 95–108.

Huang Yongnian 黄永年. "'Jie-Hu,' 'Zhejie,' 'Zazhong Hu' kaobian" "羯胡"、"柘羯"、"雜種胡" 考辨 [A Critical Analysis of the Terms "Jie-Hu," "Zhejie," and "Zazhong Hu"], in *Huang Yongnian wenshi lunwenji* 黄永年文史論文集 [Collected Essays on Literature and History by Huang Yongnian], vol. 2 (Beijing: Zhonghua shuju, 2015), 384–97.

Inaba Minoru. "Arab Soldiers in Tang China at the Time of the An-Shi Rebellion," *The Memoirs of the Toyo Bunko* 68 (2010), 35–61.

Iwami Kiyohiro. "Turks and Sogdians in China during the T'ang Period," *Acta Asiatica* 94 (2008), 41–65.

Iwao Kazushi 岩尾一史. "Kodai Chibetto teikoku no gaikō to 'sangoku kaimei' no seiritsu" 古代チベット帝國の外交と「三國會盟」の成立 [The Foreign Relations of the Ancient Tibetan Empire and the Establishment of the "Three-Country Covenant"], *Tōyōshi kenkyū* 東洋史研究 72.4 (2014), 680–715.

Kasai, Yukiyo. "Uyghur Legitimation and the Role of Buddhism," in *Buddhism in Central Asia I: Patronage, Legitimation, Sacred Space, and Pilgrimage*, eds. Carmen Meinert and Henrik H. Sørensen (Leiden: Brill, 2020), 61–90.

King, Ross. Ditching 'Diglossia': Describing Ecologies of the Spoken and Inscribed in Pre-modern Korea," *Sungkyun Journal of East Asian Studies* 15.1 (2015), 1–19.

Kósa, Gábor. "Mānī on the Margins: A Brief History of Manichaeism in Southeastern China," *Locus: Revista de História, Juiz de Fora* 27.1 (2021), 61–83.

Li Yiwen 李怡文. "Shi zhi shisan shiji Zhong-Ri jiaoliu zhong de seng-shang hezuo yu 'zongjiao-shangye wangluo'" 十至十三世紀中日交流中的僧商合作與 "宗教 – 商業網絡" [Cooperation between Monks and Merchants and the "Religious-Commercial Network" in Tenth- to Thirteenth-Century Sino-Japanese Interactions], in *Songshi yanjiu zhu cengmian* 宋史研究諸層面 [Multifaceted Studies of Song History] (Beijing: Beijing daxue chubanshe, 2020), 382–405.

Lin Kuan-Chun (Lin Guanqun) 林冠群. *Yubo gange: Tang-Fan guanxi shi yanjiu* 玉帛干戈:唐蕃關係史研究 [Peace and War: Studies on Relations between the Tang and Tibetan Empires] (Taipei: Lianjing, 2016).

Lin Song 林松. "Yuanmao suishi, wenwei shizhen – dui Xi'an Huajuexiang gusi ji Wang Hong Tianbao bei bianwei zhi qianjian" 原貌雖失, 文偽史真 –– 對西安化覺巷古寺及王鋐天寶碑辨偽之淺見 [Though the Original Is Lost and the Text Is Forged, the History Is Real—My Shallow Views on the Authentication of the Ancient Mosque on Huajue Lane, Xi'an, and the Stele Attributed to Wang Hong of the Tianbao Era], *Huizu yanjiu* 回族研究 2 (1993), 45–49.

Ma Qichang 馬其昶. *Han Changli wenji jiaozhu* 韓昌黎文集校注 [Collected Works of Han Yu: An Annotated Critical Edition] (Shanghai: Shanghai guji chubanshe, 2014).

Mair, Victor H., Nancy S. Steinhardt, and Paul R. Goldin, eds. *Hawaii Reader in Traditional Chinese Culture* (Honolulu: University of Hawaii Press, 2005).

McMullen, James. *The Worship of Confucius in Japan* (Cambridge, MA: Harvard University Asia Center, 2019).

Moribe Yutaka 森部豊. "Tōmatsu Godai no Daihoku ni okeru Sogudo-kei Tokketsu to Sada" 唐末五代の代北におけるソグド系突厥と沙陀 [The Sogdian-Türks and Shatuo of Daibei in the Late Tang and Five Dynasties], *Tōyōshi Kenkyū* 東洋史研究 62.4 (2004), 660–93.

Morley, Brendan Arkell. "Poetry and Diplomacy in Early Heian Japan: The Embassy of Wang Hyoryŏm from Parhae to the Kōnin Court," *Journal of the American Oriental Society* 136.2 (2016), 343–69.

Murakami Tetsumi 村上哲見 (trans. Zhang Fang 張芳). "Abei Zhongmalü yu Tangdai shiren" 阿倍仲麻呂與唐代詩人 [Abe no Nakamaro and His Relations with Tang Poets], *Baoji wenli xueyuan xuebao* 寶鷄文理學院學報 40.6 (2020), 87–97.

Nicolini-Zani, Matteo (William Skudalek, trans.). *The Luminous Way to the East: Texts and History of the First Encounter of Christianity with China* (Oxford: Oxford University Press, 2022).

Niu Zhigong 牛致功. "An Yuanshou muzhiming zhong de jige wenti" 安元壽墓志銘中的幾個問題 [Some Questions Relating to the Entombed Epitaph of An Yuanshou], *Shixue yuekan* 史學月刊 3 (1999), 37–40.

Oh, Young Kyun. "Two Shilla Intellectuals in Tang: Cases of Early Sino-Korean Cultural Connections," *T'ang Studies* 23–24 (2005–06), 119–47.

Orzech, Charles D. "Esoteric Buddhism in the Tang: From Atikūta to Amoghavajra (651–780)," in *Esoteric Buddhism and the Tantras in East Asia*, eds. Charles D. Orzech *et al*. (Leiden: Brill, 2011), 263–85.

Orzech, Charles D. *Politics and Transcendent Wisdom: The Scripture for Humane Kings in the Creation of Chinese Buddhism* (University Park, PA: Pennsylvania State University Press, 1998).

Park, Hyunhee. *Mapping the Chinese and Islamic worlds: Cross-cultural Exchange in Pre-modern Asia* (Cambridge: Cambridge University Press, 2012).

Pelliot, Paul. "Des Artisans Chinois à la Capitale Abbasside en 751–762," *T'oung Pao* 26 (1928), 110–12.

Peterson, Charles A. "P'u-ku Huai'en and the T'ang Court: The Limits of Loyalty," *Monumenta Serica* 29 (1970–71), 423–55.

Pinker, Steven. *The Better Angels of Our Nature: Why Violence Has Declined* (New York: Viking, 2011).

Pollock, Sheldon. *The Language of the Gods in the World of Men: Sanskrit, Culture, and Power in Premodern India* (Berkeley: University of California Press, 2006).

Pulleyblank, Edwin G. "The Background and Early Life of An Lu-shan" (University of London: Ph.D. dissertation, 1951).

Reischauer, Edwin O., trans. *Ennin's Diary: The Record of a Pilgrimage to China in Search of the Law* (New York: Angelico Press, 2020 [1955]).

Reischauer, Edwin O. *Ennin's Travels in T'ang China* (New York: Angelico Press, 2020 [1955]).

Rong Xinjiang 榮新江. *Zhonggu Zhongguo yu Sute wenming* 中古中國與粟特文明 [Medieval China and the Civilization of the Sogdians] (Beijing: Sanlian, 2014), 79–113.

Schaeffer, Kurtis, Matthew T. Kapstein, and Gray Tuttle, eds. *Sources of Tibetan Tradition* (New York: Columbia University Press, 2013).

Schafer, Edward H. *The Golden Peaches of Samarkand: A Study of T'ang Exotics* (Berkeley: University of California Press, 1963).

Schottenhammer, Angela. "Yang Liangyao's Mission of 785 to the Caliph of Baghdād: Evidence of an Early Sino-Arabic Power Alliance?", *Bulletin de l'École Française d'Extrême-Orient* 101 (2015), 177–241.

Sen, Tansen. *Buddhism, Diplomacy, and Trade: The Realignment of Sino-Indian Relations, 600–1400* (Honolulu: University of Hawaii Press, 2003).

Sen, Tansen. "Relic Worship at the Famen Temple and the Buddhist World of the Tang Dynasty." In *Secrets of the Fallen Pagoda: Treasures from Famen Temple and the Tang Court*, edited by Alan Chong (Singapore: Asian Civilisations Museum, 2014), 27–49.

Shang Yongliang 尚永亮. "Tang Suiye yu Anxi sizhen bainian yanjiu shulun" 唐碎葉與安西四鎮百年研究述論 [A Survey of Research on Tang Suyab and the Four Garrisons of Anxi during the Past Hundred Years], *Zhejiang daxue xuebao* 46.1 (2016), 39–56.

Silverstein, Adam. "From Markets to Marvels: Jews on the Maritime Route to China ca. 850–ca. 950 CE," *Journal of Jewish Studies* 58.1 (2007), 91–104.

Skaff, Jonathan Karam. "Barbarians at the Gates? The Tang Frontier Military and the An Lushan Rebellion," *War and Society* 18.2 (2000), 23–35.

Smits, Ivo. "Reading the New Ballads: Late Heian *kanshi* poets and Bo Juyi." In *Wasser-Spuren. Festschrift für Wolfram Naumann* (Wiesbaden: Harrassowitz, 1997), 169–84.

Solonin, Kirill. "The Formation of Tangut Ideology: Buddhism and Confucianism." In *Buddhism in Central Asia I: Patronage, Legitimation, Sacred Space, and Pilgrimage*, edited by Carmen Meinert and Henrik Sørensen (Leiden: Brill, 2020), 123–24.

Sørensen, Henrik H. "Esoteric Buddhism in the Nanzhao and Dali Kingdoms (ca. 800–1253)." In *Esoteric Buddhism and the Tantras in East Asia*, edited by Charles D. Orzech, Henrik H. Sorensen, and Richard K. Payne (Leiden: Brill, 2011), 379–92.

Steinhardt, Nancy Shatzman. *China's Early Mosques* (Edinburgh: Edinburgh University Press, 2015).

Tackett, Nicolas. *The Destruction of the Medieval Chinese Aristocracy* (Cambridge, MA: Harvard University Asia Center, 2014).

Takata Tokio. "Multilingualism in Tun-huang," *Acta Asiatica* 78 (2000), 49–70.

Takata Tokio. "A Note on the Lijiang Tibetan Inscription," *Asia Major* 19 (2006), 161–70.

Takata Tokio. "Tibetan Dominion over Dunhuang and the Formation of a Tibeto-Chinese Community," *BuddhistRoad Paper* 6.1, *Special Issue: Central Asian Networks. Rethinking the Interplay of Religions, Art and Politics Across the Tarim Basin (5th–10th c.)*, ed. Erika Forte (2019), 85–106.

Taylor, Keith W. *The Birth of Vietnam* (Berkeley: University of California Press, 1983).

Tor, D.G. "The Islamization of Central Asia in the Sāmānid Era and the Reshaping of the Muslim World," *Bulletin of SOAS* 72.2 (2009), 279–99.

Vaissière, Étienne de la (trans. James Ward). *Sogdian Traders: A History* (Leiden: Brill, 2005).

Von Glahn, Richard. *The Economic History of China: From Antiquity to the Nineteenth Century* (Cambridge: Cambridge University Press, 2016).

Wade, Geoff. "An Early Age of Commerce in Southeast Asia, 900–1300 CE," *Journal of Southeast Asian Studies* 40.2 (2009), 221–65.

Wade, Geoff. "Islam across the Indian Ocean to 1500 CE." In *Early Global Interconnectivity across the Indian Ocean World, Volume II*, edited by Angela Schottenhammer (Cham: Palgrave, 2019), 85–138.

Wang Rui 王睿. *Tangdai Suteren Huahua wenti shulun* 唐代粟特人華化問題述論 [A Study on the Question of Sogdian Sinicization in the Tang] (Beijing: Shehui kexue wenxian chubanshe, 2016).

Wang Xiaofu 王小甫. *Tang, Tufan, Dashi zhengzhi guanxi shi* 唐、吐蕃、大食政治關係史 [A History of Political Relations between the Tang, Tibetan, and Arab Empires] (Beijing: Beijing daxue chubanshe, 1992).

Wang, Zhenping. *Ambassadors from the Islands of Immortals: China-Japan Relations in the Han-Tang Period* (Honolulu: University of Hawaii Press, 2005).

Wang Zhongshu 王仲殊. "Jing Zhencheng yu Abei Zhongmalü, Jibei Zhenbei" 井真成與阿倍仲麻呂·吉備真備 [Jing Zhencheng, Abe no Nakamaro, and Kibi no Makibi], *Kaogu* 考古 6 (2006), 60–65.

Weinstein, Stanley. *Buddhism under the T'ang* (Cambridge: Cambridge University Press, 1987).

Wright, Arthur F. "Buddhism and Chinese Culture: Phases of Interaction," *Journal of Asian Studies* 17.1 (1957), 17–42.

Xiang Da 向達. *Tangdai Chang'an yu xiyu wenming* 唐代長安與西域文明 [Tang Chang'an and the Civilization of the Western Regions] (Shanghai: Xuelin chubanshe, 2017 [1933]).

Xue Chen. "Age of Emperors: Divisible Imperial Authority and the Formation of a 'Liao World Order' in Continental East Asia, 900–1250," *Journal of Song-Yuan Studies* 49 (2020), 45–83.

Yang, Shao-yun. *Early Tang China and the World, 618–750 CE*, Elements in the Global Middle Ages (Cambridge: Cambridge University Press, 2023).

Yang, Shao-yun. *Frontiers of the Tang and Song Empires* (StoryMap). First published online in 2020.

Yang, Shao-yun. "Letting the Troops Loose: Pillage, Massacres, and Enslavement in Early Tang Warfare," *Journal of Chinese Military History* 6 (2017), 1–52.

Yang, Shao-yun. "'Stubbornly Chinese?' Clothing Styles and the Question of Tang Loyalism in Ninth-Century Dunhuang," *International Journal of Eurasian Studies* (*Ouya xuekan* 歐亞學刊) 5 (2016), 152–87.

Yang, Shao-yun. "Tang 'Cosmopolitanism': Toward a Critical and Holistic Approach," *Modern Asian Studies* (forthcoming).

Yang, Shao-yun. "Unauthorized Exchanges: Restrictions on Foreign Trade and Intermarriage in the Tang and Northern Song Empires," *T'oung Pao* 108 (2022), 588–645.

Yang, Shao-yun. *The Way of the Barbarians: Redrawing Ethnic Boundaries in Tang and Song China* (Seattle: University of Washington Press, 2019).

Yang, Shao-yun. "'What Do Barbarians Know of Gratitude? The Stereotype of Barbarian Perfidy and Its Uses in Tang Foreign Policy Rhetoric," *Tang Studies* 31 (2013), 28–74.

Yu, Peng. "Revising the Date of Jewish Arrival in Kaifeng, China, from the Song Dynasty (960–1279) to the Hung-wu Period (1368–98) of the Ming Dynasty," *Journal of Jewish Studies* 68.2 (2017), 369–86.

Zhang Xiaogui 張小貴. *Zhongguo huahua xianjiao kaoshu* 中國華化祆教考述 [A Study of Sinicized Zoroastrianism in China] (Beijing: Wenwu chubanshe, 2010).

Zhang Yanyu 張艷玉. "Tangdai Lingzhou Kangshi jiazu kaolun" 唐代靈州康氏家族考論 [A Study of the Kang Clan of Lingzhou in the Tang], Hexi *xueyuan xuebao* 河西學院學報 34.6 (2018), 70–75.

Acknowledgments

I would like to thank Geraldine Heng, Michael Höckelmann, and two anonymous reviewers for their helpful comments on earlier drafts of this essay.

Cambridge Elements ☰

The Global Middle Ages

Geraldine Heng
University of Texas at Austin

Geraldine Heng is Perceval Professor of English and Comparative Literature at the University of Texas, Austin. She is the author of *The Invention of Race in the European Middle Ages* (2018) and *England and the Jews: How Religion and Violence Created the First Racial State in the West* (2018), both published by Cambridge University Press, as well as *Empire of Magic: Medieval Romance and the Politics of Cultural Fantasy* (2003, Columbia). She is the editor of *Teaching the Global Middle Ages* (2022, MLA), coedits the University of Pennsylvania Press series, RaceB4Race: Critical Studies of the Premodern, and is working on a new book, Early Globalisms: The Interconnected World, 500–1500 CE. Originally from Singapore, Heng is a Fellow of the Medieval Academy of America, a member of the Medievalists of Color, and Founder and Co-director, with Susan Noakes, of the Global Middle Ages Project: www.globalmiddleages.org.

Susan Noakes
University of Minnesota, Twin Cities

Susan Noakes is Professor and Chair of French and Italian at the University of Minnesota, Twin Cities. From 2002 to 2008 she was Director of the Center for Medieval Studies; she has also served as Director of Italian Studies, Director of the Center for Advanced Feminist Studies, and Associate Dean for Faculty in the College of Liberal Arts. Her publications include *The Comparative Perspective on Literature: Essays in Theory and Practice* (co-edited with Clayton Koelb, Cornell, 1988) and *Timely Reading: Between Exegesis and Interpretation* (Cornell, 1988), along with many articles and critical editions in several areas of French, Italian, and neo-Latin Studies. She is the Founder and Co-director, with Geraldine Heng, of the Global Middle Ages Project: www.globalmiddleages.org.

About the Series

Elements in the Global Middle Ages is a series of concise studies that introduce researchers and instructors to an uncentered, interconnected world, c. 500–1500 CE. Individual Elements focus on the globe's geographic zones, its natural and built environments, its cultures, societies, arts, technologies, peoples, ecosystems, and lifeworlds.

Cambridge Elements ☰

The Global Middle Ages

Printed in the United States
by Baker & Taylor Publisher Services